OAK LAWN PUBLIC LIBRARY

3 1186 Y0-BRW-767

Black Magic and Witches

Fact or Fiction?

Other books in the Fact or Fiction? series:

Black
Magic and
Witches

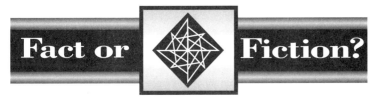

Fact or Fiction?

Tamara L. Roleff, *Book Editor*

Daniel Leone, *President*
Bonnie Szumski, *Publisher*
Scott Barbour, *Managing Editor*

OPPOSING
VIEWPOINTS®
SERIES

Greenhaven
Press®

THOMSON
————————
GALE

OAK LAWN LIBRARY

OCT - 9 2003

San Diego • Detroit • New York • San Francisco • Cleveland
New Haven, Conn. • Waterville, Maine • London • Munich

THOMSON

GALE

© 2003 by Greenhaven Press. Greenhaven Press is an imprint of The Gale Group, Inc., a division of Thomson Learning, Inc.

Greenhaven® and Thomson Learning™ are trademarks used herein under license.

For more information, contact
Greenhaven Press
27500 Drake Rd.
Farmington Hills, MI 48331-3535
Or you can visit our Internet site at http://www.gale.com

ALL RIGHTS RESERVED.
No part of this work covered by the copyright hereon may be reproduced or used in any form or by any means—graphic, electronic, or mechanical, including photocopying, recording, taping, Web distribution or information storage retrieval systems—without the written permission of the publisher.

Every effort has been made to trace the owners of copyrighted material.

Cover credit: © Richard Falco/Black Star Publishing/PictureQuest

LIBRARY OF CONGRESS CATALOGING-IN-PUBLICATION DATA
Black magic and witches / by Tamara L. Roleff, book editor.
p. cm. — (Fact or fiction?)
Includes bibliographical references and index.
ISBN 0-7377-1319-4 (pbk. : alk. paper) —
ISBN 0-7377-1318-6 (hardback : alk. paper)
1. Witchcraft—Juvenile literature. 2. Magic—Juvenile literature. [1. Witchcraft. 2. Magic.] I. Roleff, Tamara L., 1959– . II. Series: Fact or fiction? (Greenhaven Press)
BF1566 .B533 2003
133.4'3—dc21   2002000378

Printed in the United States of America

Contents

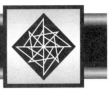

Foreword

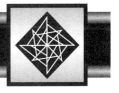

"There are more things in heaven and earth, Horatio, than are dreamt of in your philosophy."
—William Shakespeare, *Hamlet*

"Extraordinary claims require extraordinary evidence."
—Carl Sagan, *The Demon-Haunted World*

Almost every one of us has experienced something that we thought seemed mysterious and unexplainable. For example, have you ever known that someone was going to call you just before the phone rang? Or perhaps you have had a dream about something that later came true. Some people think these occurrences are signs of the paranormal. Others explain them as merely coincidence.

As the examples above show, mysteries of the paranormal ("beyond the normal") are common. For example, most towns have at least one place where inhabitants believe ghosts live. People report seeing strange lights in the sky that they believe are the spaceships of visitors from other planets. And scientists have been working for decades to discover the truth about sightings of mysterious creatures like Bigfoot and the Loch Ness monster.

There are also mysteries of magic and miracles. The two often share a connection. Many forms of magical belief are tied to religious belief. For example, many of the rituals and beliefs of the voodoo religion are viewed by outsiders as magical practices. These include such things as the alleged Haitian voodoo practice of turning people into zombies (the walking dead).

There are mysteries of history—events and places that have been recorded in history but that we still have questions about today. For example, was the great King Arthur a real king or merely a legend? How, exactly, were the pyramids built? Historians continue to seek the answers to these questions.

Then, of course, there are mysteries of science. One such mystery is how humanity began. Although most scientists agree that it was through the long, slow process of evolution, not all scientists agree that indisputable proof has been found.

Subjects like these are fascinating, in part because we do not know the whole truth about them. They are mysteries. And they are controversial—people hold very strong and opposing views about them.

How we go about sifting through information on such topics is the subject of every book in the Greenhaven Press series Fact or Fiction? Each anthology includes articles that present the main ideas favoring and challenging a given topic. The editor collects such material from a variety of sources, including scientific research, eyewitness accounts, and government reports. In addition, a final chapter gives readers tools to analyze the articles they read. With these tools, readers can sift through the information presented in the articles by applying the methods of hypothetical reasoning. Examining these topics in this way adds a unique aspect to the Fact or Fiction? series. Hypothetical reasoning can be applied to any topic to allow a reader to become more analytical about the material he or she encounters. While such reasoning may not solve the mystery of who is right or who is wrong, it can help the reader separate valid from invalid evidence relating to all topics and can be especially helpful in analyzing material where people disagree.

Introduction

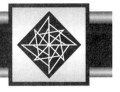

"You shall not suffer a witch to live." (Exodus 22:18)

Witches have had a negative image for hundreds of years. Raymond Buckland, a witch himself, describes the popular conception of a witch as

> an old weather-beaten crone, having her chin and knees meeting for age, walking like a bow, leaning on a staff, hollow-eyed, untoothed, furrowed, having her limbs trembling with palsy, going mumbling through the streets.[1]

There are many witches in literature and folktales that typify this image: the Wicked Witch of the West in *The Wizard of Oz* and the witch in *Hansel and Gretel*, to name a couple. In these depictions, an old hag with a pointed black hat, a flying broom, and a wart on her nose is intent on doing evil—killing Dorothy or killing and eating two young children. However, thousands of years ago, the image of witches was vastly different.

Ancient Witches

Modern witches claim that witchcraft is the world's oldest religion, predating Buddhism, Hinduism, Judaism, and Christianity. According to Starhawk, a witch who wrote *The Spiral Dance*, an introductory book on the modern version of witchcraft known as Wicca, witches believe that their craft "began more than 35 thousand years ago."[2] Back then, witches had roles similar to those of a religious leader; they were consulted when it was necessary to placate the gods or to petition for favorable weather for planting and harvesting, or good luck in hunting. They also could perform charms, magic, and spells to fulfill a supplicant's particular wish.

Witches needed the power of a deity to help them with their magic, so they directed their spells and rituals toward the Goddess and her companion, the Horned God, who oversaw the forests and the hunt. Witches led ancient hunters in ceremonies in which they acted out a successful hunt in the hopes that the Horned God would grant them similar success. For most witches, the Goddess was and continues to be their primary deity. The Goddess has three forms—the virgin, the mother, and the crone, although they are usually seen as one deity—with each form representing one of the three phases of life. The most important role of the Goddess is as the giver of life—for humans, the animals they depend on, and the land. As the giver of life, the Goddess also has the power of death by withholding life.

Early perceptions of the Goddess by nonwitches were that she could help or harm people. It was not difficult, then, to believe that the Goddess's powers were transferred to the witch who invoked her during magical rituals. In this way, witches came to be seen as having power that could be used for both good (white) magic and evil (black) magic. Witches were thought to use black magic to avenge some wrong done to them or to someone who came to them asking for help. It was believed they could cause an accident to befall their (or their friends') enemies, ruin their neighbors' crops, cause impotence, or cause farm animals to fall sick or die. People also believed that witches could produce storms, disease, and pestilence, and poison wells. As a result, while witches were respected and esteemed for the good they could do in the community, they were also a little feared for the possible harm they could cause.

As the centuries passed, people began to fear witches more than they revered them. The major factor responsible for this change in the perception of witches was the emergence of Christianity in Europe. When Christianity was a young, struggling religion, it did not have the necessary clout to squash pagan religions, so the church coexisted with paganism. In fact, the church incorporated many pagan festivals into the church calendar to persuade people to convert to Christianity. The Roman festival Saturnalia, for example, became Christmas Eve, even though biblical accounts of Jesus' birth indicate it occurred in late summer or early fall. Samhein, a Celtic festival marking the new year on October 31, was transformed into All Hallow's Eve, with the following day designated All Saints' Day to honor the dead.

Despite these attempts by the church people continued to follow old traditions, even as they converted to Christianity. As the church gained strength, its leaders saw their authority was being threatened by pagan practices. Therefore, they set out to demolish all other religions, including witchcraft.

The persecution began as early as the third century A.D., when the Romans ordered that witches who caused someone's death through witchcraft were to be burned alive. Edicts outlawing pagan beliefs, practices, rituals, and magic first appeared in 428 A.D. The death penalty was imposed on anyone who confessed to or was convicted of practicing witchcraft. Although the church and various secular authorities passed several decrees denouncing witchcraft and authorizing capital punishment for witches, few prosecutions of witchcraft actually took place until the fourteenth century. Even when prosecutions did take place, most punishments only involved performing acts of penance.

The edicts failed to eradicate witchcraft, so church officials then tried to convince people that witches did not have magical powers. At the turn of the tenth century, a church document known as the *Canon Episcopi* claimed that witches did not exist at all. It explained that those who claimed to fly through the air on broomsticks were hallucinating; those who believed such tales were deluded by the devil. The canon warned that anyone who believed such things was also guilty of heresy.

In the early Middle Ages, the church changed its stance concerning witchcraft. The existence of witches was accepted once again, but the church now argued that those who practiced witchcraft were heretics. According to the church, any religion that did not involve the worship of the One True God was evil. Any evil religion, must, by definition, worship the devil, who is evil incarnate. Because witches worshiped the Horned God, the church claimed that witchcraft was actually devil worship. Furthermore, leaders of the church began to assert that witches were the devil's agents and therefore the enemy of Christianity. Monarchs, whose own authority largely depended on church approval, went along with these assertions. Magic was especially forbidden. Historian P.G. Maxwell-Stuart writes, "As a result, the early Christian state came to treat magicians of any kind and their clients as potential trouble-makers or even enemies."[3]

The first witch to be executed under the new strictures was burned to death in 1275. The woman confessed (most likely under torture) that she had had sexual intercourse with an evil spirit, which resulted in the birth of a monster. She added that she fed the monster babies that she had kidnapped during her nightly excursions. Stories like this one were readily believed by church and government officials as well as common people.

The Burning Times

By the mid–fifteenth century, the witch hysteria in Europe had begun in earnest. Those most vulnerable to accusations of witchcraft were old women who had little value or influence in their community. But women who were healers or midwives were also susceptible to charges of witchcraft, since many of their practices, such as gathering strange plants and herbs and making potions, had similarities with witchcraft. In a time when little was known about health and hygiene and women routinely died during childbirth, healers and midwives were in a no-win situation. The recovery of someone who was terribly ill and the death of a seemingly healthy patient could both result in charges of witchcraft against the healer. Likewise, a midwife was at risk whether she delivered a live baby or a stillborn one. The fact that a patient recovered or a baby was born alive was often attributed to magic.

Literature of the time spread beliefs regarding witches and witchcraft. In an influential book titled *Malleus Maleficarum* (*The Witches' Hammer*), published in 1486, two Dominican monks claimed—among other things—that women who could not control their sexual desire would seek out the devil and his evil spirits, known as incubi and succubi, for intercourse. The authors, Heinrich Kramer and James Sprenger, reported that the widely held belief of witches flying through the air on their broomsticks to sabbats (midnight assemblies to pledge allegiance to the devil) was proof that demons were present on Earth. The authors also wrote that burning witches at the stake cleansed their souls of evil. *Malleus Maleficarum* was second in popularity only to the Bible during the Inquisition and became the church's official position on witchcraft. Its authors wrote, "To disbelieve in Witchcraft is the greatest of all heresies."[4]

To be accused of witchcraft led almost without exception to being convicted of being a witch. The use of torture against witches and other heretics in order to extract confessions was authorized by Pope Innocent IV in 1252. Most of the accused "confessed" immediately. Very few accused witches could withstand for more than a few minutes the pain inflicted by the rack, by flogging, by red-hot irons applied to the skin or eyes, or by thumbscrews that crushed thumbs and toes. In addition to the torture, witches were not allowed to present a defense to the tribunal nor allowed an appeal.

Witch-Hunting

Because of the danger witches presented to Christianity, church officials believed it was necessary to find and execute all witches. Toward that end, witch-hunters continually devised new methods for determining if the accused was indeed a witch. One practice was known as "witch swimming." The accused witch was bound—right hand to left foot and left hand to right foot—and thrown into a lake or river. If the accused floated (which often happened because of the trapped air in the victim's layers of clothing), she was a witch, because, as King James I of England rationalized, the water would not accept those who had "shaken off them the sacred water of baptism."[5] If the accused sank, then, she was innocent and was entitled to a Christian burial. Occasionally, the accused witch's family would be permitted to tie a rope around her waist so that, if she sank, they could drag her out, preferably before she drowned.

Before a suspected witch was subjected to torture, the authorities often stripped and shaved the accused from head to toe to look for a witch's mark—a mole, wart, or other body blemish said to be a sign of allegiance to the devil. It was believed that a witch felt no pain if her witch's mark was pricked. As a result, women were often stabbed all over their bodies in an attempt to find the witch's mark. Moreover, some witch-hunters deliberately deceived the witch tribunals by using daggers with retractable blades. Matthew Hopkins, a witch-hunter in England, "stabbed" accused witches with his retractable bodkin; to all appearances, the blade entered the flesh of the witch, yet the victim seemed oblivious to the pain, a sure sign of guilt.

One reason witch-hunters were inclined toward such deceptions was that witch-hunting was a lucrative business. Not only were witch-hunters paid for finding witches, but those convicted of witchcraft forfeited all their possessions to the state. During the 1620s, for example, the prince-bishop of Bamberg, Germany, collected more than 500,000 gold florins from witches executed in his principality and another 220,000 florins from suspects in prison. Witches were also charged for all expenses incurred for their torture, trial, and execution, such as the torturer's time for flogging them in jail, for the use of thumbscrews and other torture devices, even for the ropes and stakes used when they were burnt. Since accused and convicted witches were sometimes held in jail for weeks or months awaiting trial and execution, they were also charged for having their broken bones set and having salves applied after their torture.

Witch hysteria in a particular area would begin after one person was named as a witch, often after some kind of natural disaster or upon the arrival of a professional witch-hunter. Under torture, the accused witch would implicate others, who in turn would name even more people as witches. In this way, a single accusation would ripple out until sometimes all the women—and at least some of the men—in an entire town were named as witches. Then the hysteria would move on to another town, where the process was repeated.

Sometimes a local nobleman or church official would step in to stop the witch-hunt before it engulfed the entire population; other times, the authority figure would actively encourage the witch-hunts. For example, Prince-Bishop Johann Georg executed six hundred witches in Bamberg, while his cousin, Philip Adolf von Ehrenberg, prince-bishop of Würzburg, burned nine hundred witches, many of whom were children. Von Ehrenberg's chancellor noted that among the victims were "300 children of three or four years who are said to have intercourse with the devil. I have seen children of seven put to death, and brave little scholars of ten, twelve, fourteen."[6] Despite a decree by Holy Roman Emperor Ferdinand II, that opposed the torture by the two prince-bishops, the persecution did not end until Georg and von Ehrenberg died in the early 1630s.

In England, the witch hysteria never reached the frenzy it did on the Continent. The Inquisition, the Catholic Church's official mechanism for rooting out heretical behavior like witchcraft, did not extend to the island nation. Still, Parliament passed laws against witchcraft in 1542, 1563, and 1604, and by the time witch-hunting ended in England, one thousand accused witches had been executed there.

The reign of terror against witches lasted for several centuries, but by the end of the 1600s the hysteria was abating. Officials—religious and governmental—started becoming alarmed at the large number of people who were being executed for witchcraft. They began to confront the possibility that the witch trials were a mistake. In addition, although the witch trials might have generated income for the rulers in a particular region, overall, the trials and persecutions were bad for the economy. In Arras, France, for example, almost the entire village was charged with witchcraft, which frightened off villagers and tradesmen in nearby towns. In addition, lenders were refusing to extend credit to merchants in Arras, who might at any moment be accused of witchcraft and have their business and personal goods confiscated. The loss of trade threatened the economic survival of Arras until the duke of Burgundy intervened and ordered all accused witches released from prison.

The Salem Witch Trials

Just as the witch-hunts in Europe were winding down, the witch hysteria crossed the Atlantic Ocean and began spreading in England's American colonies. From the landing of the *Mayflower* in 1620 until 1725, about 350 New Englanders were accused of witchcraft. The largest witch-hunt occurred in Salem, Massachusetts, a small town of about 550 people. There, 185 were accused of witchcraft in less than one year. More than half of the thirty-five witches executed in New England were convicted of witchcraft in Salem.

Salem's witch troubles began in the home of Samuel Parris, the town's pastor. Parris's nine-year-old daughter, Betty, and his eleven-year-old niece, Abigail Williams, were often in the care of Tituba, a slave woman from Barbados. It is believed that Tituba taught the young girls and their friend Ann Putnam about voodoo, magic, and fortune-telling. When Abigail saw a coffin (signifying death) in her homemade crystal ball, she began having fits. Then Betty also had fits and convulsions. The fits started in January 1692 and lasted, off and on, for months. Parris brought in doctors and ministers who examined the girls but could find no natural cause for their condition. The Reverend John Hale, who witnessed the girls' strange actions, described them: "Their arms, necks and backs were turned this way and that way, and returned back again, so as it was impossible for them to do of themselves, and beyond the power of any epileptic fits, or natural disease to effect."[7] Eventually, authorities concluded that the girls were the victims of witchcraft.

Soon, other girls in the village were displaying signs that they were bewitched. They claimed they were being choked by invisible hands; were pinched, pricked, and prodded by invisible spirits; saw spirits in the room with them; experienced loss of memory, appetite, hearing, speech, and sight; and suffered convulsions, fits, and catatonia. Under pressure from village leaders, the girls named the witches who were tormenting them: Sarah Osborne, Sarah Good, and Tituba. All three women fit the typical profile of accused witches—they were all "different" in some way and as such were outcasts in society. Tituba was a black slave who openly admitted to practicing witchcraft. Good was an independent and mean-spirited woman who supported herself and her daughter by begging, which led the villagers to believe that she was being punished by God for some unknown action. Osborne had offended her former in-laws, the Putnams, by contesting her husband's will. She had also lived with her second husband—her former indentured servant—before marrying him. In addition, none of the women attended church, a shortcoming the villagers found extremely serious.

Osborne and Good both indignantly denied the allegations, but Tituba enthusiastically gave details of her witchcraft and magic abilities. The alarmed villagers realized they had a serious problem on their hands and immediately jailed all three women to await trial. Meanwhile, more children, and even adults, were claiming that they were bewitched, and the accusations of witchcraft against Salem villagers spread. Among the accused were Dorcas Good, Sarah Good's five-year-old daughter; Martha Corey, a respected but outspoken woman; Rebecca Nurse, an elderly woman whose family was feuding with the Putnams; and George Burroughs, the former minister of Salem who was accused of leading the witches' coven there. Salem's religious and political leaders believed it was necessary to root out and destroy witches wherever they may be, so the three girls—Betty, Abigail, and Ann—were sent to neighboring towns. They accused people in more than twenty nearby villages of practicing witchcraft.

The witch trials began in Salem in May 1692. Those who

refused to confess were subjected to torture, and if torture failed to produce a confession, the judges looked for other evidence, such as witch's marks. The most damning evidence of all, though, was the so-called spectral evidence—claims that the spirits of accused witches were tormenting the girls. According to one account of Martha Corey's trial, "When [Corey] wrung her hands [the girls] screamed that they were being pinched; when she bit her lips, they declared that they could feel teeth biting their own flesh."[8]

The first convicted witch was hanged on June 8. Good was hanged with four others a month later, on July 19. Not all the convicted witches were hanged. Osborne died while in prison. Tituba, who confessed to being a witch, was spared, as were all the other accused witches who confessed their crime. Two of those convicted of being witches died in jail. Giles Corey, Martha's husband, refused to plead guilty or not guilty before the court since the state could not confiscate his estate if he did not enter a plea. In an attempt to force a confession, he was crushed to death by stones placed on his chest.

By the end of summer, the villagers had had enough of the witch hysteria and were appalled by the ever-increasing number of people—some very well respected in the community—who were being charged with witchcraft. Finally, William Phips, the governor of Massachusetts, stepped in. He dismissed the court that had tried the witchcraft cases, prohibited further arrests for witchcraft, and, in the following spring, released and granted reprieves to all the prisoners. The Salem witch hysteria ended just over a year after it started.

The last witch in England was executed in 1682; in France, in 1745; and in Germany, in 1775. The number of witches killed during what is known as the Burning Times is estimated to be between 100,000 and 2 million people, of which about 80 percent were women. As literacy spread through Europe, scholars and scientists were able to convince many more people that fears of witchcraft were unreasonable and unscientific. Official persecution of witches ended, and although some people still believed in their existence, witches and their craft largely faded into obscurity.

Modern Witchcraft

After centuries of secrecy and persecution, witchcraft came out into the open and underwent a revival. The witchcraft renaissance began in 1899 when an American folklorist named Charles Leland wrote *Aradia, or a Gospel of the Witches.* His book was a description of what he called the "Old Religion" in Italy, which combined witchcraft with Mother Goddess worship and the Roman beliefs about the goddess Diana. Two decades later, Margaret Murray, a British anthropologist, wrote *The Witch Cult in Western Europe,* in which she linked witchcraft, the Roman Diana cult, and ancient fertility beliefs. She called this faith "the ancient religion of Western Europe."[9]

Although modern-day witches embraced Murray's description of the origins of their religion, many anthropologists and religious historians have discredited it. Her work had a great influence on the times, however. For example, England finally repealed the last of its Witchcraft Acts of 1753 in 1951. This permitted Gerald Gardner to publish three years later *Witchcraft Today,* in which he announced, "What Dr. Murray and others have suggested is correct. . . . Witchcraft certainly *was* a religion, and in fact it still is. I know because I am a Witch!"[10]

In *Witchcraft Today,* followed by *The Meaning of Witchcraft* in 1959, Gardner maintained that, although witchcraft was not dead, as many believed, it was dying out as a religion. He claimed that in 1939 he had been initiated into an ancient English coven that had managed to survive through the centuries by secretly passing its rites and lore down through generations of witches.

In his books, Gardner created a new version of witchcraft that incorporated elements of the Old Religion. His books explained the meaning behind the rituals witches performed, many of which were remembered only in fragments. Gardner revised the old ceremonies by combining the fragments that were left of the old witchcraft rituals with elements designed by his friend Aleister Crowley and others. So influential was Gardner that many witches credit him with the modern founding of witchcraft, now more commonly known as Wicca.

Wiccan Beliefs

Since Gardner popularized it, Wicca has been growing rapidly. Wiccans numbered only in the thousands in the 1960s. The Witches' Voice website estimates that at the beginning of the twenty-first century there were 1 million Wiccans, witches, and neopagans in the United States and 3 million worldwide.

The rapid growth of witchcraft is affecting government policy, as Wicca is officially recognized as a religion by the U.S. government. The District Court of Virginia, the Fourth Circuit Appeals Court, and the Department of Defense have all acknowledged that Wicca is a religion and is therefore guaranteed the protections of the First Amendment. The District Court's majority opinion in *Dettmer v. Landon* (1985) ruled that Wicca

is clearly a religion for First Amendment purposes. . . . Members of the Church sincerely adhere to a fairly complex set of doctrines relating to the spiritual aspect of their lives, and in doing so they have "ultimate concerns" in much the same way as followers of more accepted religions. Their ceremonies and leadership structure, their rather elaborate set of articulated doctrine, their belief in the concept of another world, and their broad concern for improving the quality of life for others gives them at least some facial similarity [to] other more widely recognized religions.[11]

As a result of this ruling, Wiccans have been permitted since the late 1980s to practice their rituals in U.S. prisons and on military bases.

Despite the government's official recognition that Wicca is a bona fide religion, witches continue to face discrimination and harassment in the twenty-first century, usually from conservative Christians who equate witchcraft with Satanism and the occult. In response, many witches and Wiccans have formed support networks, such as the Witches Anti-Defamation League and the Covenant of the Goddess. Although some witches and covens are willing to risk ridicule and harassment by openly practicing their beliefs, others are not and therefore meet privately or in secret. Nonetheless, people of many faiths are beginning to accept Wicca as a legitimate religion.

Notes

1. Raymond Buckland, *Witchcraft from the Inside: Origins of the Fastest Growing Religious Movement in America.* St. Paul, MN: Llewellyn, 1995, p. 1.
2. Starhawk, "Witchcraft as Goddess Religion," in Elizabeth Reis, ed., *Spellbound: Women and Witchcraft in America.* Wilmington, DE: Scholarly Resources, 1998, p. 204.
3. P.G. Maxwell-Stuart, "The Emergence of the Christian Witch," *History Today,* November 2000, p. 38.
4. Quoted in Starhawk, "Witchcraft as Goddess Religion," p. 203.
5. Quoted in Time-Life Books, *Witches and Witchcraft.* Alexandria, VA: Time-Life Books, 1990, p. 62.
6. Quoted in Time-Life Books, *Witches and Witchcraft,* p. 70.
7. Quoted in Wendy Stein, *Witches: Opposing Viewpoints.* San Diego: Greenhaven Press, 1995, pp. 62–63.
8. Quoted in Time-Life Books, *Witches and Witchcraft,* p. 75.
9. Quoted in Time-Life Books, *Witches and Witchcraft,* p. 100.
10. Quoted in Buckland, *Witchcraft from the Inside,* p. 96.
11. Quoted in the Armed Forces Chaplains Board, *Wiccan Religious Background Paper,* May 1998. www.milpagan.org.

Chapter 1

Fact or Fiction?

Evidence That Witchcraft Is Destructive

Witches' Magick Is Not a Real Power

Robert Todd Carroll

Magick is the ability to change circumstances and events solely by willing it. Sympathetic magick is based on the belief that "like attracts like"—for example, sticking pins in a voodoo doll will cause pain to the person the doll represents. While the ideas of magick and sympathetic magick are appealing, such beliefs show a profound ignorance of science. Magick does not influence events; real magic is in the beauty of nature and the ability to do and see simple, everyday things. Robert Todd Carroll is a philosophy professor at Sacramento City College. He is also the author of *Becoming a Critical Thinker* and the editor of the Skeptic's Dictionary, a website promoting skeptical thinking about paranormal and supernatural phenomena (www.skepdic.com).

M agick is the alleged art and science of causing change in accordance with the will by non-physical means.

From "Magick" and "Sympathetic Magic," by Robert Todd Carroll, www.skepdic.com, April 26, 2001. Copyright © 1998 by Robert Todd Carroll. Reprinted with permission.

Magick is associated with all kinds of paranormal and occult phenomena, including but not limited to: ESP, astral projection, psychic healing, the cabala, chakras. Magick uses various symbols, such as the pentagram, as well as a variety of symbolic ritual behaviors aimed at achieving powers which allow one to contravene the laws of physics, chemistry, etc. Magick should not be confused with magic, which is the art of conjuring and legerdemain.

The religions based on the Old and New Testaments have long associated magick with false prophets, based upon the belief that Satan regularly exhibits his powers to and shares them with humans. Using powers which contravene natural forces is good if done by or through God (white magick), according to this view. Such exhibitions of divine power are called miracles. If done by diabolical forces, it is evil (black magick).

The idea of being able to control such things as the weather or one's health by an act of will is very appealing. So is the idea of being able to wreak havoc on one's enemies without having to lift a finger: just think it and thy will will be done. Stories of people with special powers are appealing, but for those contemplating becoming a magus consider this warning from an authority on the subject:

> Magick ritual (or any magick or occultism) is very dangerous for the mentally unstable. If you should somehow 'get out too far', eat 'heavy foods' . . . and use your religious background or old belief system for support. But remember too, that weird experiences are not necessarily bad experiences. [Phil Hansford, *Ceremonial Magick*]

Those are words of wisdom to live by: *the weird is not necessarily bad*. On the other hand, the weird is not necessarily good, either.

The magic of performing magicians is related to magick in that performers use tricks and deception to make audiences think they have done things which, if real, would require supernatural or paranormal powers, e.g., materializing objects such as rings or ashes, doves or rabbits. Some magicians have attributed their feats not to magic but to supernatural or paranormal powers, e.g., Sai Baba and Uri Geller.

Of course, the beauty and magic of nature has nothing to do with magick. There is the magic of the birth of a healthy child; the magic of true love. There is the magic of getting out of bed in the morning through an act of will. Unfortunately, this only seems to be magic to those who do not have this power. Those of us who can direct our bodies through acts of will too often take this power for granted. We fail to see the wondrousness of simple things, like wiping the sweat from one's brow. We take for granted the act of opening our eyes to feast on the sublimity of glaciers and oceans or the beauty of sunsets or meadows of wild flowers. These are truly magical deeds and, when contemplated, hold enough wonder to fill universes. But for many, it seems, such *real* magic will never be enough.

Sympathetic Magic

Sympathetic magic is based on the metaphysical belief that like affects like. Sympathetic magic is the basis for most forms of divination. The lines, shapes and patterns in entrails, stars, thrown dirt, folded paper, the palm of the hand (the longer the lifeline, the longer the life), etc., are believed to be magically connected to the empirical world—past, present and future. It is also the basis for such practices as sticking needles into figurines representing enemies, as is done in voodoo. The pins and needles stuck in a doll are supposed to magically cause pain and suffering in the person the doll represents.

Sympathetic magic is the basis for the claims of psychic detectives who claim that touching an item belonging to a victim gives them magical contact with the victim. Barry Beyerstein believes that sympathetic magic is the basis for many New Age notions such as "resonance," the idea that if things can be mentally associated they can magically influence each other. Beyerstein also explains many notions of graphologists as little more than sympathetic magic, e.g., the notion that leaving wide spaces between letters indicates a proneness to isolation and loneliness because the wide spaces indicate someone who does not mix easily and is uncomfortable with closeness. One graphologist claims that a person betrays his sadistic nature if he crosses his t's with lines that look like whips.

Sympathetic magic is probably the basis for such notions as karma, synchronicity, eating the heart of a brave but defeated warrior foe, throwing spears at painted animals on cave walls, wearing the reindeer's antlers before the hunt, having rape rituals to increase the fertility of the crops, or taking Holy Communion to infuse the participant with Divinity. Sympathetic magic is surely the basis for homeopathy and remote healing.

Magic Is Not Scientific

Anthropologists consider magical thinking a precursor to scientific thinking. It is indicative of a concern with control over nature through understanding cause and effect. Nevertheless, the methods of magic, however empirical, are not scientific. Such thinking may seem charming when done by our ancestors living thousands of years ago, but today such thinking may indicate a profound ignorance or indifference towards science and a testable understanding of the world. Most of us, from time to time, undoubtedly slip into this primitive mode of thinking, but a bit of reflection should wake us up to the fact that oysters are not an aphrodisiac, having a bit of good luck is not likely to influence our chances of winning the lottery that day, and stabbing a photo of an enemy is not going to hurt her. It may be true that rubbing an amulet given you by your true love makes you feel her presence, but the feeling you have, however magical it may seem, has more to do with biology and psychology than with metaphysics. And changing your name to Dirk Studmuffin will not cause the cosmos to shake, rattle and roll.

Witchcraft Is Full of Lies

David L. Brown

Witches, also known as Wiccans, use deception to remake their image so that they are acceptable to mainstream society. Witches claim that they practice good, healing magic as part of the world's oldest religion and that Wiccans are wholesome, family-oriented people. These claims are lies. Wicca is a modern religion that draws upon satanic occult rituals and ceremonies, including blood offerings and human sacrifice. Witchcraft is also a perverted sex-oriented cult whose members participate in orgies and other depraved sexual practices. Wiccans sin against God and are destined for damnation unless they repent. David L. Brown, a Baptist pastor, is the president of Logos Communication Consortium, an organization that examines historical and contemporary issues from a Christian and biblical perspective.

From "Unmasking the Truth About Witches," by David L. Brown, http://logosresourcepages.org, June 1997. Copyright © 1997 by David L. Brown. Reprinted with permission.

I have a news article in my files entitled "Witches Seek Mainstream Status." To be sure, witches are out of the broom closet and walking down main street. In fact, they are going to great lengths to sanitize their reputation and remake their image. That is easy to see when you see media articles with titles like "Witches spell it out: Don't Stereotype Us," and "I Am Not a Wicked Witch." In the process of trying to remake themselves to be acceptable to mainstream Americans they use deceptive schemes, old tricks and dirty lies to accomplish their goal. The following are but a few examples.

White-Washing the Name "Witch" by Using the Term Wiccan!

Most of today's witches prefer to be called "wiccans" instead of witches. The very name witch conjures mental images associated with evil and they want to change that. They go to great lengths to redefine themselves by using the term *wicca*. But the word *witch* comes from the Old English word *wicca* (masculine) *wicce* (feminine) which means *to practice sorcery*. In fact our English word *wicked* is from the root word *wicca* and literally means witch-like. As early as 890 A.D. the word "wiccan" was used to identify witches "in the *Laws of King Alfred*." In short, changing the name from witch to wiccan is an attempt at historical revisionism. A witch or wiccan is, by the very name, a defining word for wickedness.

Wicca: The World's Oldest Religion

Wiccans have told me over and over again that Wicca is the world's oldest religion and that Wicca is older than Christianity. Problem is, that is a lie! Aidan Kelly, Ph.D., founder of two of the largest witchcraft organizations in America exposes this myth. The write-up for his book, *Crafting the Art of Magic—Book 1*, puts it this way, *"Kelly himself wanted to be-*

lieve that Wicca was the rediscovering of ancient Goddess-worshipping people. However, his research proved that this is not the case." In fact, Gerald Gardner (1884–1964) is the inventor of the cult of Wicca. In his book, *At the Heart of Darkness*, John Parker says, *"retired (British) civil servant Gerald Brosseau Gardner, inventor of a witch cult* (was) *an old fraud."* But why would Parker say that? I'll tell you why. *"There is much evidence suggesting that Gardner concocted most of his rituals and legends from his own fertile imagination and that he promoted witchcraft for economic and sexual reasons."* The article goes on to say that any witchcraft group that claims roots prior to 1950 is highly suspect. In short, today's Wicca or witchcraft is a modern cult originating in the 1950's and can not legitimately claim to be older than Christianity.

Witches Do Not Believe in or Acknowledge the Devil/Satan

While Wicca has a modern origin, they eclectically draw upon diabolical occult information, rituals, and ceremonies from idol worshippers of the past. In fact, they use a deceptive scheme involving semantic word games to deny their involvement with the Devil and/or Satan. For instance, Wiccans will tell you that they believe in Lucifer. They claim that "he is the god of the Sun and of the Moon." However most knowledgeable Wiccans recognize that the book *La Sorciere* by French historian Jules Michelet is a major contributer to their cult (the English version is published by Citadel Press under the title *Satanism and Witchcraft*). But, here's the facts. *"Michelet's book is full of passionate, sympathetic depictions of Satan and medieval witchcraft."*

Then there is the book by Charles G. Leland, *Aradia: Gospel of the Witches*, which is another major source of Wiccan beliefs. The very first paragraph reads "Diana greatly loved her brother Lucifer, the god of the Sun and of the

Moon, the god of Light, who was so proud of his beauty, and *who for his pride was driven from Paradise."*

GOTCHA! This is a reference to Isaiah 14 in the Bible where Lucifer is expelled from the presence of God and becomes the Devil or Satan! In fact, Isaiah 14:12 (KJV) is the only passage where Lucifer is mentioned in the entire Bible. Otherwise he is called the Devil, Satan, the Dragon, etc.

But that is not the only example. In *Mastering Witchcraft: A Practical Guide for Witches,* Paul Huson makes this statement: *"This is a beginner's guide to practical witchcraft, revealing the techniques and secret workings of those who practice the black arts. It presents the first steps to becoming a witch. . . . It answers all the basic questions about spells, magical recipes, rituals, divination, covens, curses, apparatus, how to develop one's power, etc. From reciting the Lord's Prayer backward through . . . details for spells to arouse lust . . . attain vengeance."*

Speaking of vengeance, consider this ritual of wrath, *"a conjuration of the Horned One"* recorded on page 186: *"I conjure thee by Barabbas, by Satanas, by the devil cursed be! I summon thee by Barabbas, by Satanas by the devil conjured be! By the underworld itself . . ."* Need I note that Barabbas and Satanas are references to the devil who is mentioned?

Again, we see the attempt by modern witches to deny the truth. The Gospel of John 8:44 has interesting ramifications when it comes to this cover-up by witches: *"Ye are of your father the devil, and the lusts of your father ye will do. He was a murderer from the beginning, and abode not in the truth, because there is no truth in him. When he speaketh a lie, he speaketh of his own: for he is a liar, and the father of it."*

Let's move on to two more lies witches tell.

More Lies

The upside-down pentagram is satanic, not wiccan. Nothing could be further from the truth! It is well documented that in the Gardinarian and Alexandrian Wiccan cult, they use the upside-down pentagram as the symbol of Second Degree Initiation.

Wiccans only do good magic, healing magic. On numerous occasions I have been told by witches that the Wiccan Rede ("An it harm none, do what ye will") and the threefold law (evil directed at another will return threefold upon the perpetrator) hinders witches from directing magic spells or other negative actions against anyone. That just is not true! For instance, famous witch Sybil Leek published a book called the *Book of Curses*. Earlier in this article I mentioned Paul Huson's book *Mastering Witchcraft*. In it, *"full details are given for spells to . . . attain vengeance."* Cursing and vengeance are not good any way you look at it. This is just another attempt to mask the truth.

Wiccans are wholesome, family-oriented people. Witches are not the wholesome, family-oriented people they claim to be. Doreen Irvine, a practicing witch for many years, said, many *"witches were lesbians and homosexuals."* And she's right. I have a poster, letter and application in my files for, as they called it, "FAGGOT WITCH CAMP." The letter advertised the *"second annual FAGGOT WITCH CAMP, August 26–30, 1991."* This event was held at Wyalusing State Park in Prairie du Chien, Wisconsin. According to the letter, *"Our purpose in organizing this event is to gather with like-minded queer men and to explore our unique perspectives and experiences as faggot witches."* This queer event was even announced in the witch publication *Circle Network News,* Spring 1991.

Witchcraft is a perverted sex-oriented cult. According to the book, *What Witches Do,* *"Witchcraft has always been a fertility religion . . . "* and the orgy was a part of the Craft *"giving the plainer girls a chance."*

Gardinarian witch Patricia C. Crowther describes modern day witch orgies this way:

The motives of the modern witches are often thought to be questionable, and certainly a considerable element of sexuality is present at many meetings. . . . The nudity of the coven, the frantic dancing, the incense and the slightly illicit atmosphere contribute to this. . . . The binding and whipping of new initiants for "purification" purposes, for instance, is highly titillating for those with sado-masochistic tendencies . . . while 'the five-fold kiss' bestowed by the high priest or priestess on the feet, knees, genitals, breasts and lips of the new members speaks for itself. The 'Great Rite,' performed at certain ceremonies and consisting of token or actual sexual intercourse . . . is justified on the grounds that Wicca is, after all, a fertility cult. Only the high priest may initiate a female member, while the high priestess initiates the males.

One of the most important religious organizations of Neo-Paganism in America is the Church of All Worlds (CAW). . . . CAW played a key role in the 1970's in the networking of diverse Pagan and Wiccan groups. . . . Their official journal is the *Green Egg—A Journal of the Awakening Earth*. The entirety of Volume 29, No. 119, 1997 dealt with ritual sexual sado-masochism. There certainly is nothing wholesome about that!

Sexual Perversion

Then there was the case of an Ohio witch who ended up in court. A 15-year-old girl "was selected as high priestess of the cult" and he initiated her and several other teenage girls in a perverse way. The news article states, "There were candles, seances, rituals. They would have to be naked and have sex with him in order to get involved with the magic." The witch leader was charged with three counts of second degree sexual assault of a child, and two counts of sexual intercourse with a child aged 16 or older. Again, witches lie when they say they are wholesome. Sexual perversion is never wholesome!

Speaking of sexual perversion, I also have in my files a copy of a witchcraft publication that states that a well known east coast witch "transitioned" from male to female on Samhain [Halloween], October 31. What that means is that the person was born a biological male but had his sex organs surgically removed and altered to appear to be female. That IS perversion! In fact, another noted witch who has authored a best selling book on witchcraft under a female name, was born a biological male.

Sexual perversion abounds in many witch covens and organizations!

In 1991, I published a 30-page research report entitled *The Dark Side of Halloween.* In the book I quoted a former witch who said, *"Sadism was practiced frequently . . . "* Several years back I brought this up on a national talk show. When I said this, two witches who worshipped Dagon [a Philistine deity] were sitting on one side of me and a vampire on the other. The audience was peppered with witches. As soon as the words were out of my mouth there was a hot protest from the witches. In fact, since the show was not live, the witches put so much pressure on the producers that they edited out my words! They did not want the public to know about their sadistic practices. While not all witches engage in such perversions, there is a large constituency that do.

I will conclude this section by saying, there is nothing wholesome about any of these perverted sexual practices. While witches try to mask these diabolical practices, the record speaks for itself. And as Dr. Merill Unger observes, "for those who surrender to worship and serve Satan, the moral degradation and perversion is horrifying."

Blood Offerings

Witches don't believe in blood offerings, animal or human sacrifice. While many Wicca cult members offer fruit and vegetable sacrifices to their pagan gods and goddesses, blood offerings and animal or human sacrifices are a part of historic pagan and witchcraft rites. But, it is becoming increasingly frequent in the witch community today.

I have read several accounts and have recorded personal testimonies of individuals who were initiated into witchcraft that incorporated rituals using their own blood. Consider Alex Sanders (1926–1988). He is the father of Alexandrian Wicca. He was initiated into witchcraft using a blood ritual. A witch had "him stand nude in a circle with his head down. She took a sharp razor, cut his scrotum to make it bleed. . . . He was initiated as a third degree, and he became a black magickian."

There are other uses of blood as well. For instance there is a connection between blood and the witches wand. *"The most efficacious wand will be made of one of the woods sacred to the White Goddess: elderberry, willow, rowan, hazel, oak or mistletoe."* The article goes on to say that the branch is then hollowed out and *"filled with cotton wool and brought to life with three drops of the witch's own blood."*

The use of blood to facilitate power is not uncommon. One witch told me that they had anointed their divination board with their own blood so as to empower the board.

In the book *Secrets of the Occult* by C.A. Burland, it talks about groups in south Germany about 1960 who *"hunted and decapitated deer for a blood-drinking rite."* In fact, there are those who claim to be witches, even Wiccans who do that and worse today.

Consider the case of Wiccan Damien Wayne Echols. He was involved with the ritual murder of Michael Moore, Christopher Byres and Steve Branch. There are those who accused Echols of being a Satanist but Echols asserts that he is a Wiccan. In a search of his home they found a book of spells, potions and prayers which was his book of shadows.

It begins with an entry stating *"all rites are to be performed within a nine-foot circle."* The article goes on to say, *"following that, there is a ritual to be used for 'improving' the memory, which includes using the 'heart, eye or brain of a lapwing or plover (birds) and hanging it on one's neck."*

Wiccans loudly protest when things like this are pointed out. And while I am sure that not all witches are involved in blood sacrifices there are those who are. Further, the originator of the Wiccan Cult, Gerald Gardner, was involved in human sacrifice. Here is what is recorded. *"The group was deadly serious about their secret ritual. . . . But to be 100 per cent effective there would have to be a human sacrifice."* One of the coven members volunteered.

> The coven was also known to use an hallucinogen. . . . Having formed their magic circle in the depths of the forest, the group, who were naked, made a line and held hands and then danced furiously around a small bonfire, chanting incantations. . . . They performed the rite with such vigour that one or two of them fainted, a not uncommon experience when a serious amount of power and energy is aroused by the perfomance of ritual. The old volunteer duly collapsed and died, and it is not known whether it was from an overdose of mushrooms, over-exhaustion or the cold. *The great sacrifice had been made and the potency of their magic . . . enhanced.*

Historically, human sacrifice has been associated with witchcraft. Anyone who is intellectually honest will admit that. But it seems that some Wiccans are finally coming out of the closet and preparing the way for the acceptance of human sacrifice within their ranks. In fact, a major Wiccan periodical carried an article titled "Sacrifice: An Elevation." In this article Nasira Alma states, *"We cannot be 'above' sacrifice, human or other. . . . Divinors foresaw events by noting the manner of the victim's fall, the twitching of his limbs, and how his blood spurted. . . . Sacrifice is the law of our nature. It maintains the balance between the inner and the outer, the physical and the spiritual, the Divine and the human."*

Witches desperately want public acceptance! As you have seen, many will lie in an effort to get it. A massive nationwide disinformation campaign has been mounted to convince people that their beliefs and practices are normal and acceptable. This report has been prepared to unmask just a few of their deceptive schemes, old tricks and dirty lies.

We are warned in the Bible, Ephesians 5:11, *"And have no fellowship with the unfruitful works of darkness, but rather reprove them."* There is good reason for that warning because the power behind witchcraft and the occult is demonic power. In Acts 16:16–18 we see that the psychic powers of the young girl were demonic in origin. In fact, in the article entitled "Communicating with the Departed," the author admits to what we know to be demon possession when she says *". . . for the spirit to be contacted actually enters the Wytche's body . . ."* Is it any wonder that Paul says of Elymas the sorcerer, *"O full of all subtlety and all mischief, thou child of the devil, thou enemy of all righteousness, wilt thou not cease to pervert the right ways of the Lord?"* Acts 13:10. The same can be said of any witch today.

The Problem with Witchcraft and the Occult

It is important that people understand that there are two sources of wisdom available to mankind — God's wisdom and the Devil's wisdom. We see this in James 3:15–17 *"This wisdom descendeth not from above, but is earthly, sensual, devilish. For where envying and strife is, there is confusion and every evil work. But the wisdom that is from above is first pure, then peaceable, gentle, and easy to be entreated, full of mercy and good fruits, without partiality, and without hypocrisy."*

Demonic wisdom (Lucifer's or the Devil's wisdom), that wisdom that "descendeth not from above, is characterized as being earthly, sensual and devilish." God's wisdom on the other hand is said to be pure, peaceable, gentle, etc. In short, there are two very different kinds of wisdom with two very different outcomes.

Biblical Christianity is the manifestation of God's wisdom from above. Wicca, witchcraft, paganism, Satanism, etc. are manifestations of the devil's wisdom from beneath.

We are encouraged to seek God's wisdom and power. And, in fact the Bible outlines the means we are to use in seeking to access that wisdom and power.

How to Tap into God's Wisdom and Power

The wisdom that God commends may be accessed through . . .

• Prayer

James 1:5 If any of you lack wisdom, let him ask of God, that giveth to all men liberally, and upbraideth not; and it shall be given him.

• Bible study and meditation

Psalms 19:7 The law of the LORD is perfect, converting the soul: the testimony of the LORD is sure, making wise the simple.

Colossians 3:16 Let the word of Christ dwell in you richly in all wisdom; teaching and admonishing one another in psalms and hymns and spiritual songs, singing with grace in your hearts to the Lord. (See also 2 Peter 3:15–16 & 2 Timothy 3:16–17)

Hebrews 4:12 For the word of God is quick, and powerful, and sharper than any twoedged sword, piercing even to the dividing asunder of soul and spirit, and of the joints and marrow, and is a discerner of the thoughts and intents of the heart.

• Wise counsel

Proverbs 1:5 A wise man will hear, and will increase learning; and a man of understanding shall attain unto wise counsels:

Proverbs 12:15 The way of a fool is right in his own eyes: but he that hearkeneth unto counsel is wise.

On the other hand, there are ways people attempt to tap into demonic wisdom as well. But the Bible warns us that God condemns and forbids seeking after demonic wisdom. This is clearly articulated in Deuteronomy 18:9–12 where we are told not to learn to imitate the detestable ways of the occult. Divination, sorcery, witchcraft, mediums, necromancy, casting spells and more are said to be an *abomination to the Lord.*

How People Attempt to Access Demonic Wisdom

• Divination/fortunetelling

Divination is the act of attempting to prophesy (forecast future events) or human character through occult means by making use of certain omens or divination tools such as tarot cards, tea leaves, Ouija board, astrology, palmistry, scrying devices (crystal balls, mirrors, crystals, etc.). The method of divination often changes but the spirit and force behind it remains the same . . . a demon spirit (Acts 16:16–18).

• Sorcery/magick

Sorcery is the act of attempting to contact, manipulate or control people, spirits, animals, plants, the elements (earth, air, fire, water) through occult rituals, ceremonies, objects (amulets, talismans, charms, etc.). Though magic may "work," the power behind magic is demonic and those who practice magic are the enemies of righteousness. (Acts 13:6–10)

• Spiritism/necromancy

Spiritism or necromancy is an occult activity grounded in the belief that through certain persons acting as mediums or channels (psychics, necromancers, channelers, etc.) the dead or the spirit world can be contacted and hidden information can be acquired from those contacted. Trances and seances are often used by the medium. The power behind this activity is demonic. This activity is forbidden by the Lord. 1 Chronicles 10:13, *"So Saul died for his transgression which he committed against the LORD, even against the word of the LORD, which he kept not, and also for asking counsel of one that had a familiar spirit, to inquire of it."* (1 Sam. 28:7 gives the context).

In fact, by the personal testimony of neo-pagans, Wiccans and Satanists I have personally talked to, and as recorded in the hundreds of books as well as in the files that I have in my archive, they ALL (pagans, Satanists, Wiccans and other occult groups I have not even mentioned), without exception, attempt to secure their wisdom through one or more of the occult means I have just mentioned.

We are to order our lives by the wisdom of God. That is the wisdom revealed in the Bible. This is the wisdom of Jesus Christ. *"Jesus saith unto him, I am the way, the truth, and the life: no man cometh unto the Father, but by me."* John 14:6

We are to reject the wisdom from beneath, the wisdom of the devil, the wisdom of Wicca. The wisdom of witchcraft is the wisdom of the damned . . . Revelation 21:8 *"But the fearful, and unbelieving, and the abominable, and murderers, and whoremongers, and sorcerers, and idolaters, and all liars, shall have their part in the lake which burneth with fire and brimstone: which is the second death."*

If you are involved in witchcraft or other occult practices you are sinning against the Lord God of Heaven and you are destined for damnation in the Lake of Fire. But, if you repent of your sins and call upon the Lord Jesus Christ to forgive your sins and save your soul Heaven can be your destiny. John 3:16–18, 36:

> For God so loved the world, that he gave his only begotten Son, that whosoever believeth in him should not perish, but have everlasting life. For God sent not his Son into the world

to condemn the world; but that the world through him might be saved. He that believeth on him is not condemned: but he that believeth not is condemned already, because he hath not believed in the name of the only begotten Son of God. . . . He that believeth in the Son hath everlasting life: and he that believeth not the Son shall not see life; but the wrath of God abideth on him.

Witchcraft Threatens Youth

Jason Barker

Television shows and movies are increasingly marketing the occult to youth. In addition, teens are able to easily buy books that explain how they can become witches. These books include popular spells that appeal to teens. As a result, witchcraft is on the rise among teens. Christian parents should be concerned about the increasing popularity of Wicca among teens. Jason Barker worked with the Watchman Fellowship, a Protestant countercult ministry, for many years before establishing the Southwest Institute of Orthodox Studies in Arlington, Texas.

The occult is becoming an increasingly common component of television programs oriented towards youth. The increased exposure of witchcraft and other occultic practices is increasing the acceptance of these practices by youth as ex

Excerpted from "Youth and the Occult," by Jason Barker, *Watchman Expositor,* www.watchman.org, 1998. Copyright © 1998 by Watchman Fellowship, Inc. Reprinted with permission.

citing, exotic alternatives to mainstream religion (particularly Christianity).

An informal study of local teenagers by the *Lexington (Kentucky) Herald-Leader* in 1997 showed that "Most said there's a subculture at nearly every school that includes Anne Rice–influenced gothic kids, faux vampires and outcast kids who dabble in the occult. After all, in the Bible Belt, what could be more shocking than experimenting with witchcraft, vampirism or Satanism?"[1] The study concluded that most signs of teenage involvement in the occult (such as satanic symbols on book bag or bumper sticker) are merely a superficial sign of temporary rebellion against societal boundaries. . . .

Witchcraft

One of the most notable practices being marketed to youth is witchcraft, or magic, frequently in the form of Wicca. The 1996 movie *The Craft* picked up on the trend, inaccurately presenting a coven of high school students who use magick to fulfill their personal desires.

Silver RavenWolf, self-described as one of the foremost witches in the United States, accurately describes witchcraft as "an earth-centered religion focused on raising an individual's spirituality. WitchCraft [*sic*] is not, nor was it ever, a vehicle for Satanic worship."[2] Affiliated with Goddess worship, witchcraft is an experiential religion in which rituals and the celebration of seasonal festivals are intended to enhance an individual's self-awareness and increase the power that person has to influence her destiny without outside influence. Displaying the syncretism that is so much a part of current New Age and occult practices, RavenWolf teaches that the techniques of witchcraft can be used in any religious tradition.[3]

Witchcraft is on the rise among young people, particularly high school and college-age females. This author had a student in a technical writing class at a major state university who, for a semester project, developed a manual for the Wicca coven in which she was involved. This project was merely part of the trend of publishing books that market witchcraft to teens. For example, *Inside a Witches' Coven* attempts to address the concern students seeking to find or join a coven, describing the beliefs, styles and customs that a witch may choose to consider.

Marketing Geared Toward Teens

The most significant new publication for youth is *Teen Witch: Wicca for a New Generation* by Silver RavenWolf. Its colorful cover, with a painting depicting four adolescent females (and one male) provocatively posing in front of a full moon rising over a fog-shrouded grove, clearly is intended to attract its target audience (a free poster of the cover is available for purchasers "while supplies last"[4]). Showing the popularity of the book, *Teen Witch* was sold out in all but one of five major chain bookstores visited by the author while searching for a copy; he bought the last copy in the fifth store.

RavenWolf is well aware that many parents, and particularly Christians, object to witchcraft. For this reason, the first section of the book is addressed to parents and claims (in bold print), "This is an okay book for your children to read. There's nothing bad in here, and maybe the book will help you understand why WitchCraft is one of the fastest growing religions in America."[5] She further advises parents, "For pity's sake, don't 'tell' [your children] what religion is and is not. Let them discover spirituality for themselves."[6]

What is it that teens are supposed to discover for themselves? In its own words, *Teen Witch* was written so that

Now, for the first time, [teens] can explore what it's like to be a real Witch with a book written especially for you.

- Find out how the Wiccan mysteries can enhance your life

- Begin your journey with the Teen Seeker Ceremony

- Combine common herbs from the supermarket to make your magickal formulas

- Create your own sacred space

- Read true stories of Wiccan teens

- Work magick with real spells

- Learn the Craft techniques for gaining love, money, health, protection, and wisdom

- Discover how to talk to friends, parents, and other people about your involvement with WitchCraft.[7]

The contents of *Teen Witch* are clearly intended to appeal to disillusioned teens who "sense an aliveness or 'presence' in nature. . . . They share the goal of living in harmony with nature, and they tend to view humanity's 'advancement' and separation from nature as the prime source of alienation. They see ritual as a tool to end that alienation."[8] Teens who read *Teen Witch* are thus hoping to learn how to manipulate natural forces to end their sense of loneliness and alienation from society and the world.

The spells described in *Teen Witch* constitute a thorough inventory of the concerns of American teens. There are numerous spells for receiving money, a "Hot Wheels" spell for receiving a car, a "Crabby Teacher" spell, a spell for passing exams, a prayer for "Owl Wisdom" (divine assistance in planning for the future), a "Doodle Bug Love Spell" for raising self-esteem, a "Do You Like Me?" spell, a "Call Me" spell (as well as a "Don't Call Me" spell), and even a "Little Bo Peep Spell to Find Lost Objects."

The book concludes with a plan for teens to win approval for their witchcraft from parents. RavenWolf advises teens to link philosophical and theological difficulties to a need for the existence and practice of witchcraft. Knowing that some parents "won't get past their fear" and accept witchcraft (she says that such parents "aren't behaving in an adult manner"[9]), RavenWolf tells the children of parents who "still won't budge [to] pray. The Mother will hear you."[10]

The involvement of American youth in the occult is, for lack of a better description, broad but shallow. In other words, occultic activity by teens has been observed across the country in such areas as Nashua, New Hampshire; Dallas; Burlington, Wisconsin; Salt Lake City; and Los Angeles. At the same time, it is only a small percentage of youth who are engaging in occultic practices; RavenWolf states that teen witches will lose many of their friends, particularly Christians (she sarcastically describes these as "real winners"[11]). Goths (both the philosophical Goths, and those who use the movement as a springboard for occultism) register similar complaints.[12]

Despite the relatively small number of youth currently involved in occultic activity, the growing movement should be a source of concern for Christians.

Notes

1. Barbara Isaacs, "Most Teens Don't Cross the Line, Say Students," *Lexington Herald-Leader,* April 13, 1997 [Online]. URL http://www.kentuckyconnect.com/heraldleader/news/970413/ff2line.html.
2. Silver RavenWolf, "A Note to the Parents on Teen WitchCraft," *Llewellyn's New Worlds of Mind & Spirit,* October 1998, 2.
3. Ibid.
4. *Llewellyn's New Worlds of Mind & Spirit,* October 1998, 5.
5. Silver RavenWolf, *Teen Witch: Wicca for a New Generation,* St. Paul, MN: Llewellyn, 1998, xiii.
6. Ibid.
7. Frontispiece, *Teen Witch: Wicca for a New Generation,* St. Paul, MN: Llewellyn, 1998.

8. Margot Adler, quoted in Bob and Gretchen Passantino, *When the Devil Dares Your Kids,* Ann Arbor, MI: Servant, 1991, 57.

9. RavenWolf, *Teen Witch,* 231.

10. Ibid., 233.

11. RavenWolf, *Teen Witch,* 233.

12. "Mall Gothics," *New Hampshire Weekly,* n.d. [Online]. URL http://www.geocities.com/BourbonStreet/2672/gothic/goffic3.html.

Harry Potter Books Lure Children to Witchcraft

Jacqui L. Komschlies

Books about the supernatural are fascinating to children; however, they contain dangers which often go unnoticed. Children who devour books about the supernatural, such as the Harry Potter books about witchcraft, often crave their own mystical experiences. The Harry Potter books teach many lessons that are problematic for Christians; foremost among them is the issue of magic. Harry Potter and his friends use magic to achieve their will; Christians know that it is not their will, but God's will, that should be done. Many children who read the Harry Potter books will want to become witches themselves, a practice that is condemned by the Bible. Parents who allow their children to read these books should discuss with their children how the plots, characters, and actions are inconsistent with God's views. Jacqui L. Komschlies is a writer based in Wisconsin.

From "Where's the Warning Label for Harry Potter?" by Jacqui L. Komschlies, *Lutheran Parent*, November/December 2000. Copyright © 2000 by Northwestern Publishing House. Reprinted with permission.

Nearly everything for kids, from cough medicine to jacks, comes with a warning label. "May cause vomiting" or "Danger—choking hazard." I always read the labels. Sometimes the risks outweigh the benefits, and the product goes back on the shelf. Other times, knowing my kids are unlikely to be harmed, I decide the risks are minimal, and I put the product in my shopping cart.

Looking back, I wish some of the books I read as a child had come with a warning label. From about age 10 to my early 20s, the supernatural fascinated me. I devoured stories about wizards and magic, power and adventure, to the point of reading three or four books a week. I craved mystical experiences of my own.

On the outside, I was a normal kid. I had been confirmed and went to church nearly every week. My report cards were always straight A's. On the inside, however, I was sliding downhill into a world that was leading me away from my Savior—God. The supernatural realm was taking over my thoughts. I couldn't stop imagining the spirits and the powerful gods and goddesses I was reading about. They were in my dreams. And, finally, one day they started speaking to me.

I cried out to God in fear, and he rescued me. I stood teetering at the brink of the pit, and he pulled me back into his arms. I tremble now when I realize how close I came to losing my faith and being trapped in the darkness of unbelief. I know I am forgiven—Jesus died for those sins too—but I hope other children will avoid my mistakes.

In regard to issues not directly forbidden in Scripture, the Lutheran church teaches discernment, not censorship. But I cringe when I see Christian kids choosing the same genre of mystical books that I did. To make matters worse, those types of books, which I once had to search for, are now available everywhere. The Harry Potter series by J.K. Rowling, about a boy chosen for Hogwarts School for Witchcraft and Wizardry, are by far the most popular. The *Washington Times*, June 6, 2000, reported that more Harry Potter books had been sold than any other children's books in history. For its initial release, Scholastic Books printed 3.8 million of the fourth book, *Harry Potter and the Goblet of Fire.* And it expects to be reprinting for many years to come.

Most children who read Harry Potter books may be unaffected, but some may start down the same path I traveled. For them, Harry Potter will start a hunger for more of the same. With hundreds of choices of books, games, TV shows, and even an upcoming Harry Potter movie, there will be plenty of opportunities to nurture their interest in wizards and witchcraft, and it will grow.

Problems with Harry Potter

As Christian parents, we need to talk to our children and point out a few problems with Harry Potter mania. First, the books teach that good magic defeats bad magic, one of the foundational beliefs of pagan, or earth-based, religions such as Wicca. Wiccans believe that a supernatural force or power exists in everything. By learning the right rituals or spells, or by seeking help from spirits, that same power can be harnessed and used to accomplish the will of the individual witch. Only evil people use the power to practice black magic.

As Christians, we know that real supernatural power comes from only two places: God and Satan. God's power can't be manipulated—only Satan allows that deception. We pray "Thy will be done," not "My will be done." But people who practice authentic witchcraft use power directly from the devil, even when their intentions are good. Where does that leave Harry Potter?

Second, Harry attends classes at Hogwarts School for Witchcraft and Wizardry, and the reader accompanies him. Harry is an ordinary schoolkid, a nice boy, and his class work sounds like fun—much more fun than most of us had in school. Who wouldn't rather learn spells, divination, potions, and sorcery instead of grammar and arithmetic? When you look at Harry's list of classes, it sounds eerily familiar. Compare Harry's strange interests in the supernatural with Deuteronomy 18:10–12: "Let no one be found among you who . . . practices divination or sorcery, interprets omens, engages in witchcraft, or casts spells, or who is a medium or spiritist or who consults the dead. Anyone who does these things is detestable to the LORD."

The reader learns the supernatural arts with Harry. Harry sometimes studies magic that is silly and cute; there is an obvious innocence to it. But mix up his "Draught of Living Death," and you risk real hallucinogenic nightmares. Pay attention in divination class, and you'll also learn actual fortune-telling techniques. Stop in at a large bookstore or go to Amazon.com with a list of Harry's textbooks, such as *Standard Book of Spells, A History of Magic,* and *The Dark Forces—A Guide to Self-Protection.* You can go home with *The Book of Spells, The History of Magic: Including a Clear, and Precise Exposition of Its Procedure, Rites and Mysteries,* and *Battling Dark Forces—A Guide to Psychic Self-Defense.* These are real books about witchcraft and sorcery; there is nothing innocent about their purpose or their subject matter.

And if reading about witchcraft prompts you to go one step further down that dark slope, type in "How can I become a witch?" at Askjeeves.com or another Internet search engine and learn step-by-step how to become a modern-day pagan, including how to properly worship the horned god. Over three thousand Web sites offer information on pagan practices, with more under development. This isn't pretend.

This is the dark undertow of the occult, and it can pull under anyone who lacks firm footing on the bedrock of God's Word. Even now, reading Harry Potter books for research, I feel the tug of its current.

Muggles

Third, parents need to be ready to explain the attitude toward "muggles"—people who don't believe in the world of witches or spurn it as evil. In the Harry Potter books, muggles are cruel, boring, and stupid people who couldn't recognize decency if they tried. For example, Harry's aunt hides him in a closet when company comes. His birthday goes uncelebrated, and his uncle strictly forbids contact with anyone from the wizard school. When Harry's best friend calls during summer vacation, Harry's uncle furiously bellows, "How dare you give this number to people—people like you!"

As muggles are portrayed, we would have to agree with the way magical people feel about them. And yet, when we think about it, we are the muggles of our real world. The author is talking about people like us. If we found someone we loved practicing witchcraft, we would want to help that person put a stop to such pagan practices, wouldn't we? Galatians 5:20,21 warns us that those who practice witchcraft will not inherit the kingdom of God. If a children's book portrayed homosexual acts as exciting, fun, and beneficial, and those who opposed them were presented as brutal hate mongers, would we buy such a book for our kids?

The Bible speaks out against sorcery and witchcraft. It admonishes us to stay away from every kind of evil. But nowhere does it say, "Thou shalt not read Harry Potter books." Still, the early Christians burned their books of witchcraft after hearing and believing the gospel. Would fantasy books about witchcraft have gone into the fire too?

Finally, consider our children's Christian witnessing. My daughter might read Harry Potter books without harm, but what about her weaker friend? By giving Harry Potter to my child, might I cause another child to stumble?

We usually make very informed choices of what to feed our bodies. With God's help, we can make informed choices of what to feed our minds too. And, thankfully, he can make even our bad decisions work out for good.

So, is it okay for your children to read Harry Potter books? That's between your family and God. If you choose to go ahead, read the books together and have discussions about how the characters, plots, and situations don't fit with God's view. When my daughters have reached a fairly high level of Christian maturity, I want them to read the first Harry Potter book—not for entertainment, but for help in recognizing the dangers and learning discernment of their own.

Wiccans Should Not Be Permitted to Serve in the U.S. Military

Robert L. Maginnis

Although Wicca is a valid religion recognized by the U.S. government, its practice should not be permitted by members of the armed forces of the United States. Wiccans would negatively affect military readiness because their values and beliefs are antithetical to those shared by most service members. Most Wiccans believe in a radical feminist worldview and participate in deviant sexual behavior. Furthermore, most Wiccans are pacifists, a belief that does not belong in an organization whose sole purpose is warfare. Robert L. Maginnis retired from the U.S. Army as a lieutenant colonel. He is a policy expert on military readiness for the Family Research Council, a Washington, D.C.–based think tank that promotes traditional family values.

From "Brewing Up Trouble: Wicca and the U.S. Military," by Robert L. Maginnis, www.frc.org, June 1999. Copyright © 1999 by Family Research Council, Inc. Reprinted with permission.

Wicca received official recognition as a religion in 1996 from the Department of Defense. Today, there are at least five officially recognized military Wiccan congregations.[1] The Pentagon should withdraw recognition of Wicca for readiness reasons.

Objections to the military's recognition of Wiccans fall in two categories: One, any fringe religion will now have to be granted special benefits by DOD; two, Wicca will undermine readiness factors such as military values, adherence to norms, willingness to kill, and recruitment and retention among the majority who hold a generally theistic worldview and regard witchcraft as an abomination.

The presence of minority religious views is not at issue in this controversy. Christians have served in the military in good faith with Muslims and Jews. These religions share a monotheistic and creationist consensus about the "law of nature and nature's God," as understood by the signers of the Declaration of Independence. Because Wicca represents a direct challenge to this widely shared theism, it would work against military discipline, order, and readiness.

Wicca represents a direct affront to Christian and Jewish teaching. The Bible condemns all forms of witchcraft and sorcery throughout the Old and New Testaments (Leviticus 19:26, 31 and 20:6; Deuteronomy 18:10–12; 2 Kings 17:10–17; 21:1–6; and 23:4–7, 24–25; 2 Chronicles 33:6; Acts 13:6–12 and 16:16–18; Galatians 5:19–21; and Revelation 9:20–21).

U.S. Representative Bob Barr, a Georgia Republican, has asked the services to stop sanctioning the practice of witchcraft on military bases. Barr argues that allowing such celebrations sets "a dangerous precedent" that could lead to "all sorts of bizarre practices being supported by the military under the rubric of religion."[2] Already, DOD has granted special benefits to other unconventional religious groups. Military members of the Native American church, for example, can legally use the illegal hallucinogenic drug peyote in their on-base religious ceremonies.[3]

Military Support of Religion and Wicca

The U.S. military has always supported religion. On July 29, 1775, George Washington "established the [chaplain] corps behind the idea that chaplains brought with them morality and ethics, and that was important in dealing with the forces."[4] Today, the chaplain corps seeks to meet the needs of a very diverse uniformed population.

In 1998, the Defense Manpower Data Center found that most servicemembers identify with the Christian faith: 330,703 Roman Catholic; 252,855 Baptist (not including Southern Baptist); 43,056 Lutheran; 40,053 Methodist; 25,833 Southern Baptist Convention; 62,063 Protestant but with no denominational preference; and 96,259 labeling themselves Christians with no denominational preference. Twenty percent (283,836) have "no religious preference." Other religious preferences include Judaism (3,913), Muslim (4,080) and Buddhism (2,228). No Wiccans were identified.[5]

Military regulations provide a process for religious groups without chaplains to gain access to base facilities for the purpose of conducting services. The qualification process requires that the group must be a recognized religion, military members must request the service and there must be evidence that assigned chaplains cannot meet the "specific theological/denominational requirements of [the] group."[6]

The U.S. government has recognized Wicca and has given it tax-exempt status as a religious organization. In fact, according to one website, "Wiccan priests and priestesses have been given access to penitentiaries."[7]

In August 1997, Wicca "high priest" David Oringderff, with the Sacred Well Congregation of San Antonio, helped set up the military's first Wicca Open Circle at Fort Hood near Austin, Texas. The Wicca Open Circle at Fort Hood has perhaps 300 members, about 100 of whom attend regularly.[8] Oringderff has helped set up congregations at four other bases as well.[9]

The Army defends its decision to support Wicca. *U.S. News & World Report* explains,

> For today's heterogeneous U.S. Army, the practice is basically business as usual. 'As far as we are concerned, they are a religious organization providing for the spiritual needs of our soldiers,' says Lt. Col. Benjamin Santos, Fort Hood spokesman, explaining the Army's decision to sanction the practice on bases.[10]

Navy Captain Russell Gunter, executive director of the Armed Forces Chaplains Board at the Pentagon, also supports Wiccans at Fort Hood. The military is obligated, said Gunter, to respect the religious needs of its members without passing judgment.[11]

Background of Wicca

Witchcraft, also known as Wicca, the craft, or the craft of the wise, is a religion with roots in the ancient pagan religions of northern Europe. Modern witchcraft is a reconstruction of the older versions, based on writings by anthropologist Margaret Murray (1863–1963)—*The Witch-Cult in Western Europe* (1921) and *The God of the Witches* (1933)—and by British civil servant and world traveler Gerald Gardner (1884–1964)—*Witchcraft Today* (1954) and *The Meaning of Witchcraft* (1959).[12]

Llewellyn's 1999 Magickal Almanac explains,

> Wicca, as you practice the religion today, is a new religion,

barely fifty years old. The techniques you use at present are not entirely what your elders practiced even thirty years ago. Of course, threads of 'what was' weave through the tapestry of 'what is now.' . . . [I]n no way can we replicate to perfection the precise circumstances of environment, society, culture, religion and magick a hundred years ago, or a thousand. Why would we want to? The idea is to go forward with the knowledge of the past, tempered by the tools of our own age.[13]

"Contemporary witchcraft is so diverse and eclectic . . . that it is extremely difficult to accurately identify and define. In fact, it is almost impossible to state that all witches believe 'this or that,'" writes Craig Hawkins in the *Christian Research Journal*.[14]

Wiccan Beliefs

Radical Feminism. Danya Ruttenburg wrote in the April 1998 *Sojourner* (a feminist magazine),

[M]any feminists have certainly been attracted to paganism—the theological framework behind energy-channeling called magic or witchcraft. Women who practice paganism often describe it as a potent means of aligning their spiritual practice with their political beliefs.

Though the modern practice has deep roots in a number of ancient traditions, the neo-pagan movement was initiated in England in the 1950s. It took hold in America in two separate, parallel movements—both as part of the non-Western spirituality explosion of the late 1960s, and with the concurrent development of goddess consciousness, in radical separatist feminism.[15]

Russ Wise, with the Dallas-based Probe Ministries, adds,

In the world of witchcraft the goddess is the giver of life. Witchcraft holds a pantheistic view of God. God is nature. Therefore, God is in all things and all things are a part of God. However, this God is in actuality a goddess and predates the male God. The goddess is the giver of all life and is found in all of creation. This reshaping is nothing less than viewing man and his understanding of reality from a female-centered perspective which focuses on the Divine as being female. . . . The rise of the goddess is a direct assault on the patriarchal foundation of Christianity. This new feminist spirituality affirms bisexuality, lesbianism, homosexuality, and androgyny (through the expression of transvestitism).[16]

"The Goddess religion is a conscious attempt to reshape culture," says Starhawk, a witch who works with a Catholic priest at the Institute of Creation Spirituality.[17]

Pacifist Tendencies. A June 1999 edition of the *Washington Post* identifies Wiccans as pacifists. Despite the "many varieties of Wicca," Wiccans in general accept a basic rule: "An ye harm none, do what ye will."[18]

The Armed Forces Chaplains Board explains that many Wiccans "regard all living things as sacred" and consequently hold that the destruction of human and animal life is wrong. Others believe that "as Nature's way includes self-defense, they should participate in wars that they conscientiously consider to be just."[19]

Nonviolence, however, is the first principle of Wicca, according to a Wicca website:

The harm which is to be regarded as unethical is gratuitous harm; *war, in general, is gratuitous harm* [emphasis added], although it is ethical to defend oneself and one's liberty when threatened by real and present danger, such as defense against invasion.[20]

An article titled "Pagans in the Military" by John Machate, published by the Military Pagan Network, elaborates,

In an article by Isaac Bonewits, Archdruid of ADF (Arn Draiocht Fein), he stated:

'A "soldier", [sic] on the other hand, I perceive as a hired killer, whose primary task is not the defense of his/her community, although that claim is usually made, but rather the defense of that community's political, social, religious, and economic rulers.'

This statement reflects the attitude of a lot of civilian organizations. One organization doesn't even want to allow military members to belong to their organization. We as members of the armed forces have to work, not only to convince the military that we are not 'baby killers', [sic] but the civilian pagans too. Again I quote Isaac Bonewits 'He [sic] or she will kill any man, woman, or child that he/she is ordered to kill, simply because he/she was told to do so. . . . '[21]

(Note: A witch holds pagan beliefs, but not all pagans are witches.)[22]

Ethical Relativism. The Covenant of the Goddess, one of the largest and oldest Wiccan religious organizations in North America, states that evil is subjective: "[W]hat is good for one may be evil for another and vice versa."[23]

Other examples of this relativistic view abound. Additional Wiccan websites, for instance, make the following claims:

- "Wiccans rely on their own judgement [sic] to create their own morals, and ideals. . . . We interact with our gods on a regular basis, and we take their power into ourselves during our rituals. We know and feel our Gods, so we don't believe, we know."[24]
- "Witches consider no act immoral unless it is harmful."[25]
- "Witches have no specific taboos against speaking any particular words, consensual sexual acts among individuals capable of rational consent, or breaking laws they know to be unjust."[26]

Excerpt from a pagan pledge: "May I always be mindful that I create my own reality and that I have the power within me to create positivity in my life."[27]

Wiccan Practices and More

- Magic is part of the witches' religion: "astrology, astral projection (out-of-body experiences), incantations, mediumship (channeling), necromancy, raising psychic power, (for many) sex magic, spell casting, and trance states."[28] Magic, they claim, allows them to "change our lives by spiritual . . . means. . . . We back up our actions with magical intent. It is a potent combination."[29]

- According to one witch, witches worship

> the Mother Goddess and also the Horned God. . . . Worship is often done in pairs, masculine and feminine, and the power, which is produced by magical ritual, is directed by the High Priestess for its desired purpose. . . . Covens vary in size from approximately 8 to 14 members. The High Priestess heads the coven. The High Priestess who trained her is recognized as a Queen to whom she can turn for counsel and advice.[30]

- Casting spells is "part of being a Witch," according to the Covenant of the Goddess (COG). However, COG advises that one cast spells on others "only in very limited circumstances" when "that person's . . . consent" has not been obtained—acknowledging the power which spells contain.[31]

- Sex magic, which is practiced by some witches, is the "use of sex (e.g., intercourse—actual or symbolic) within a ritual or spell-casting session to facilitate or augment the efficacy of a given magical rite. That is, sexual activities are used to accomplish the desired goal of the occultist."[32]

- The COG website indicates that witches practice necromancy, communication with the dead. Some witches "believe that the dead join the Blessed Ancestors, who watch over, protect and *advise* [emphasis added] their descendants."[33]

- Wiccan "tools" include swords, cauldrons, wands, boleens (knives used for carving and cutting magical symbols), staffs, and thuribles (incense burners).[34]

- The basic Wiccan dedication ritual states:

> I will protect and guard the Old Ways from those who would desire to destroy them. I will defend the God

and Goddess. I will work in harmony with the energies of the Earth, and the Kingdoms of Plant, Animal, Spirit, and Man, striving always for unity and balance. I will work in harmony with the elements, to understand them. I pledge myself as protector of this Earth and Keeper of the Sacred Mother. I will honor and respect my brothers and sisters in the Craft even when our paths do not join. I will respect and keep the Old Ways and the Wiccan Rede. So mote it be.[35]

Implications for Military Readiness

- Cohesive units are made of soldiers who subscribe to similar values. For the military, there are clear rights and wrongs, not maybes. Wiccans, on the other hand, are noted for their ethical relativism.

- Wiccans subscribe to a radical feminist worldview that supports sexually deviant behavior such as bisexuality and homosexuality, both of which are illegal in the military.

- A "Wiccan warrior" is an oxymoron. Wiccans tend to be pacifists, which may be all right for medics but not for infantrymen.

- The military has already allowed peyote smoking to accommodate Native Americans, and there are a growing number of cases of Muslim soldiers appealing decisions about headgear, dietary requirements and special holidays. Exceptions for every group will drain limited resources and distract from the military's primary mission of preparing to fight. The military should embrace corporate rather than individual interests.

- Today's military is overwhelmingly Christian. The Bible labels witchcraft as an abomination. Accommodating witches who engage in behaviors that are antithetical to the "law of nature and nature's God" will cause unit friction, undermine morale, and impair recruitment and retention.

Unfortunately, the modern military has embraced tolerance for virtually every bizarre practice. It's past time for Congress to exercise its constitutional obligation to stop the Pentagon's willingness to sacrifice national defense in order to accommodate political correctness. The armed forces should focus on readiness.

Notes

1. Kim Sue Lia Perkes, "Wiccans becoming more at home in military," *Dallas Morning News*, May 29, 1999, p. 1G. (Wiccans have congregations at Fort Hood, Texas; Fort Wainwright, Alaska; Fort Polk, La.; Kadena Air Base in Okinawa; and Fort Barrancas in Pensacola, Fla.)

2. "No Witching Hour for Barr," News Briefs, *Army Times*, June 7, 1999.

3. "Military OKs Using Peyote, Indians Say," Associated Press, *Dallas Morning News*, June 21, 1999. (In the April 28, 1997, edition of *Navy Times*, Karen Jowers reports, "In 1994, Congress passed a law allowing authorized American Indians to use the drug [peyote] in religious ceremonies. Since last summer, defense officials have been writing regulations that would set out guidelines for the military.")

4. Marcia Jackson, "Chaplain Corps celebrates 221st birthday," *ArmyLINK News*, July 18,1996, http://www.dtic.mil/armylink/news/Jul1996/a19960718chap.html.

5. Jack Weible, "A Smorgasbord of Religions," *Army Times*, July 13, 1998.

6. "Distinctive Faith Group Leaders, Certification Process," U.S. Army Training Command, Fort Monroe, Virginia, http://www-tradoc.monroe.army.mil/chaplain/dsl.htm, accessed June 22, 1999.

7. "Witchcraft and Wicca," http://www.religioustolerance.org/witchcra.htm, accessed June 22,1999.

8. Perkes, *op cit.*

9. *Ibid.*

10. Joe Holley, "A genuine witch hunt," *U.S. News & World Report*, June 14, 1999, p. 27.

11. Perkes, *op cit.*

12. Craig S. Hawkins, "The Modern World of Witchcraft," *Christian Research Journal*, Winter/Spring 1990, p. 8.

13. Silver RavenWolf, cited in *Llewellyn's 1999 Magickal Almanac*, Llewellyn Publications, 1998, http://www.religioustolerance. org/witchcra.htm, accessed June 22, 1999.

14. Hawkins, *op. cit.*

15. Danya Ruttenburg, "Witchy Woman: Paganism, Politics, and Spiritual Healing," *Sojourner*, April 1998, p. 25.

16. Russ Wise, "The Goddess and the Church," Probe Ministries, 1997, http://www.probe.org/docs/godd-chu.html.

17. Quoted by Wise, *ibid.*

18. Hanna Rosin, "An Army Controversy: Should the Witches Be Welcome?" *Washington Post*, June 8, 1999.

19. The Armed Forces Chaplains Board, "Wiccan Religious Background Paper," submitted to the Chief Chaplains of the Armed Services in May 1998, http://www.milpagan.org/files/ AFCB_Wicca_paper.htm.

20. "Wiccan Ethics—Basic Principles of the Craft," http://home1. gte.net/buckmstr/wiccanethics.htm, accessed June 22, 1999.

21. John Machate, "Pagans in the Military," http://milpagan.org/ articles/pagmilt.htm, accessed June 22, 1999.

22. "The Grove: What is a Pagan? What is a Witch?" http://www. apocalypse.org/pub/u/hilda/ddtmqa.html, accessed June 22, 1999.

23. "Witchcraft: Commonly-Asked Questions, Straightforward Answers," Covenant of the Goddess, http://www.cog.org/ wicca/faq.html, accessed June 22, 1999.

24. "Calhoun's Wiccan FAQ," http://www.geocities.com/SoHo/ Lofts/3156/wicca.html, accessed June 22, 1999.

25. "The Grove—What is a Pagan? What is a Witch?" *op. cit.*

26. *Ibid.*

27. "Circle Sanctuary—A Pledge to Pagan Spirituality," http:// www.circlesanctuary.org/contact/PSApledge.html, accessed June 22, 1999.

28. Hawkins, *op. cit.*

29. "Witchcraft: Commonly-Asked Questions, Straightforward Answers," *op. cit.*

30. Lady Rhiannon, "Gardnerian Wicca," http://160.149.101.23/chap/relpractice/other/gwicca.htm, accessed June 24, 1999.

31. "Witchcraft: Commonly-Asked Questions, Straightforward Answers," *op. cit.*

32. Hawkins, *op. cit.*

33. "Witchcraft: Commonly-Asked Questions, Straightforward Answers," *op. cit.*

34. "The Witches' League for Public Awareness—The Tools of Witchcraft," http://www.celticcrow.com/basics/tools.html, accessed June 22, 1999.

35. "The Witches' League for Public Awareness—Dedication Ritual," http://www.celticcrow.com/basics/dedication.html, accessed June 22, 1999.

Chapter 2

Fact or Fiction?

Evidence That Witchcraft Is Benign

Magick Works

Janet Brennan

Wiccan rituals are sacred ceremonies wherein witches gather to pray to deities and perform magick. Witches believe magick is a normal power that they find within themselves and in the energies present in fire, water, plants, stones, colors, sound, and movement. Spells, whether simple or complicated, work in achieving a witch's desire, although sometimes not in ways visualized by the witch. Herbs, candles, and incense all work to help direct the energy toward achieving the witch's goal, but the most important element of any magick is the witch's will and desire. Janet Brennan is a frequent contributor to *Fate* magazine

The name of the coven is the Iseum of Hidden Mysteries, but nothing looks mysterious about the antique red farmhouse that is its headquarters.

As I enter through the back door, I'm warmly greeted by coven leaders Julie and Lawrence, an ordinary-looking married couple. I instantly feel at ease as their gentle hound strolls over for a pat and a black-velvet kitten scampers after

From "The New Face of Witchcraft," by Janet Brennan, *Fate*, August 1999. Copyright © 1999 by Fate Magazine. Reprinted with permission.

a shoelace. But this Sunday afternoon promises to be far from ordinary for me, for I am attending my first pagan ritual, performed by a coven of witches.

The word *pagan* means "country-dweller"—an appropriate description for Julie and Lawrence, who live in the thick pine woods 30 miles from the coast of Maine. They are members of The Fellowship of Isis, a pagan church with about 14,000 members worldwide who focus their worship on Egyptian deities. But while Julie feels an affinity for Egypt, she actually considers herself a "hedge witch"—one who practices an eclectic mixture of Druidism, Native American shamanism, and many other forms of pagan worship. "We don't feel we need to reinvent the wheel," Lawrence explains. "We use whatever works," Julie adds.

While Julie was brought up Catholic, Lawrence was exposed to many world religions as a child. He later became involved in the ecology movement, which drew him to the nature worship of paganism. He and Julie met in the U.S. Coast Guard, and today, they are legal clergy in the church headquartered at their farm, where they teach meditation and visualization techniques—both essential components of witchcraft magic.

Most covens will not admit outsiders to their rituals, but I was granted entry on one condition: I would have to attend as a full participant, not merely as an observer. I had agreed to their terms, but I was nervous about what I had gotten myself into. I already knew that, contrary to popular myth, pagans are not devil worshippers and don't offer living sacrifices. But would I be expected to dance naked under the full moon or something?

Once in a Blue Moon

My apprehension melts away as the other group members arrive: a quiet, pretty girl, a genial young man, an ebullient widow in her fifties, and her more subdued friend. Their occupations range from construction worker to personnel director of a school district. This very normal, casually dressed group of people gathers in the cozy living room for Julie to explain the day's ritual.

The date is January 31, 1999—a special day for witches. Not only is it an Esbat (a full moon), it is also a rare blue moon (the second full moon in the month). The power of the full moon will be used in the ritual, but the ceremony will primarily focus on celebrating Imbolc, the ancient holiday marking the first stirrings of spring. Imbolc occurs on February 2, but to take advantage of the full moon and the weekend, the coven is celebrating a few days early. The ritual will not take place in moonlight, but rather at 2:30 in the afternoon—after all, some of the witches have Super Bowl parties to attend.

Julie explains that the changing seasons can mirror the changes in our own lives, making it a good time to end an old project and begin something new. Lawrence passes out pens and paper, and Julie instructs us to write, "I release all that is written here" on one piece, followed by something in our lives we want to end like a health problem or souring relationship. On another slip of paper we write "I welcome all that is written here," followed by any new activity or condition we would like to have in our lives, whether it be better health, a new boyfriend, or a new job.

Julie passes out some prayers she has written for the ceremony, and dons a purple robe. Lawrence remains in jeans and a sweater; he later explains that he doesn't bother with "ritual clothes," but he does refrain from wearing things to the ceremony that he feels may carry negative energies, such as his watch, wallet, or money.

We adjourn to the ritual space in the hayloft of their barn. The orange glow of a kerosene heater and sunlight streaming through skylights make the room bright and cheery. Egyptian paintings on the walls and gold stars swirling in spirals across the blue ceiling lend the barest touch of mystery. Four low tables serve as altars, holding candles, Egyptian statues, crystals, and seashells.

First, Lawrence "purifies" each of us by *smudging*—waving a feather through incense smoke. Julie marks our foreheads with a dab of saltwater. Thus we are purified with the four elements: earth (represented by the salt), air (the feather), fire (incense), and water.

A typical pagan ritual usually involves consecrating sacred space ("casting the circle"), invoking the spirits of the four directions or the elements of earth ("calling the quarters"), praying to the deities, and sharing a consecrated meal. Lawrence leads us in a few minutes of deep breathing and meditation to quiet and center ourselves. Then, Julie casts the circle. As we stand in a circle, she walks behind us, holding her "athame" (ritual knife) at waist level, casting away negative energies. With the tip of her knife, she draws a "circle of energy" in the air, which will contain our psychic powers. Next, the group "calls the quarters." Facing each direction in turn, four members read Julie's prayers. Each prayer invokes the spirits of the north, south, east, and west.

Now, it is time to do a little magic. Julie invokes the Goddess and Lawrence the God, asking them to bless our new endeavors. One by one, each coven member approaches the northern altar and says, "I release all that is written here." Each member then lights his or her "old things" paper in a candle flame and drops the burning paper into a small cauldron. In turn, each person says, "I welcome all that is written here," burning the paper on which his or her desired goal was written.

The next part of the ceremony is either called "bread and ale" or "cakes and wine." In a ritual sharing of nature's bounty, we pass a chalice of white grape juice around the circle. Each person offers the cup to his or her neighbor in the circle and says, "May the blessings of the Goddess be upon you." The recipient answers "Blessed be," takes a sip from the cup, then offers it to the next person. A loaf of bread is likewise passed. "May the blessings of the God be upon you," we say. Some giggling ensues when people have trouble ripping off pieces of the crusty loaf. Amid the playfulness, I feel a real sense of communion with these erstwhile strangers.

We casually pass the chalice and loaf around the circle for those who have actual hunger or thirst rather than just a symbolic need. We chat for several minutes about plans to decorate the temple. Then it is time to end the ceremony. Still standing in our circle, we meditate for a few moments to send our psychic energies back into the Earth. Our priest and priestess thank the Goddess and God, and we offer prayers of thanksgiving and farewell to the spirits of the four quarters. Julie declares the circle opened, and with the words "Merry meet, and merry part, and merry meet again," our short Imbolc ritual is over. . . .

It's a Magical World

One misconception about witches is that they get magic powers from the devil. This is uninformed propaganda, for the simple reason that witches don't believe in Satan. While some witches think evil entities exist, all reject the notion that wrongdoing is caused by people succumbing to the temptation of a devil. Rather, evil is an individual failing. "With the Craft, you are responsible for your own actions, and can blame neither man nor God for your mistakes," says Pennsylvania coven leader Silver RavenWolf, author of *Teen Witch* and other books.

So, if they're not consorting with the devil, where do witches get their magical power? From within themselves.

Witches learn to access their divine natures by practicing meditation and visualization. Witches also derive magic through use of the energies present in colors, sound, movement, fire, water, plants, and stones.

The non-witch world views magic as something supernatural, but to witches magic is simply natural. "You can't separate magic from life," says Arwen Evenstar, a former New York City news photographer and teacher now practicing as a Gnostic pagan in Maine. Witches, so closely attuned to nature and with the ability to see God/Goddess in everything, easily appreciate the magic of life itself. But they also use ritual magic—that is, spell-casting.

A spell can be as simple as lighting a candle while visualizing your desire, or so complicated that it requires pages of incantations, specific oils and incense, certain colored candles, and careful timing with the moon phase, day, and planetary hour. But does magic work? Yes it does, witches say, though sometimes in unexpected ways.

"I have never seen anything so remarkable that the Fox network would want to air it," says Acadia Elle, a thirty-something witch who cares for her special-needs child. "But I have seen it transform a frantic mind into a calm and peaceful one."

For Galadrielle, a 32-year-old witch and mother of four teen witches, magic is much more dramatic. "I have only had need in my life on one occasion, when my husband and I were buying our dream house," she recalls. "We saved like crazy for the down payment, but we found out that we needed twice the amount we had. I knew our situation was bleak.

"I turned to magic with a money spell. I put my heart and soul into it. The next day we went to the bank and applied for the loan. Not only did they give us the money on the spot, they gave us extra so that we wouldn't use up all of our savings account and would still have money for the Christmas season! I was astonished but grateful."

Sometimes, however, magic brings unexpected bad results. "The Threefold Law, in which all magic returns to the sender three times, has rebounded on me in cases where I've done an unethical spell," admits Jane Raeburn, a 33-year-old newspaper editor and author of a book on Celtic Wicca.

Lady Crystall, a grandmother in Blaine, Washington, has a similar admission. "Most of my magic has had positive results, but there was one spell when I was still a bit new to all this that really backfired. The Rede says, 'If it harm none, do what thou will.' Well, that also means not messing with someone else's free will. I did a love spell naming a specific person. It turned out to be a real bad mistake; he became obsessed with me and abusive. It took me three and a half years to get out of that one."

Sometimes spells go wrong simply because of inexperience. "Most witches have horror stories, especially from when they were first starting out," notes LunaKala, a teen witch. "I needed a job desperately, so on the morning of an interview I did a spell. I thought I had the right incense, stones, and herbs; while I did get some of my choices right, others were not good at all. And I was too relaxed in my presentation because of casting the spell. That can be a bit disastrous. . . . During the interview I zoned out. I couldn't help it. After that embarrassment I didn't do a spell for a while until I had gained a bit more knowledge."

Wicca-Wide Web

These witches' anecdotes suggest that magic works, but we don't have to just take their word for it. Twentieth-century science provides evidence that magic is possible through a natural part of our reality, albeit an invisible one. Physicists studying the theory of quantum electrodynamics have shown that all atoms constantly send out streams of sub-atomic particles, which mingle with the streams of sub-atomic particles from other atoms, so that all matter is continually interacting with other matter and with magnetic and electrical fields. In other words, the universe is one vast web of interconnecting atoms, each affecting and being affected by the others. Wiccans say they can direct their own energy to bend that stream of ever-changing reality to their will, weaving their spells into the web of the universe.

Quantum physics provides "a scientific explanation for that which many of us have intuited over centuries," says Marilyn R. Pukkila, who teaches a course on Wicca at Colby College in Maine. "Magic is developing a consciousness of that connectedness and then using that consciousness in a conscious way. The goal is to work with energy, to bend or shape it in some fashion." In fact, the word *Wicca* is also thought to come from *wicce*, meaning "to bend."

"The herbs, candles, incense, and other tools may themselves contribute to the effect by the quality of the energies they are releasing, but it's up to the practitioner to focus the energies and direct them, being very, *very* clear about the desired outcomes," Pukkila emphasizes. "'If it harm none, do what ye will' doesn't just mean 'Do whatever you like as long as you don't hurt anyone.' One's will *must* be engaged for any effect to be achieved."

Other witches agree that willpower is an essential ingredient in magic. Galadrielle says she put her "heart and soul" into her successful mortgage-loan spell, while LunaKala made the mistake of being too relaxed with her job-interview spell. Silver RavenWolf says magic is not hocus pocus, but rather "it's hocus *focus*." Witches might be better than most people at maintaining focus, as they spend years learning meditation skills so they can clearly visualize their desired outcomes.

In addition to using their own will, witches tie into the power of a greater will—the Divine Will—by calling on the God(dess) or other spirits. "Magic is ritualized prayer," RavenWolf says, "and prayer contains more magic than you can possibly imagine."

So does magic work because of individual mental powers—will—or does it work because of divine intervention?

"No amount of magic can actually manifest change in a lasting or meaningful manner without a loving connection to the sacred," Wiccan author Phyllis Curott writes in *Book of Shadows*. "This is the secret of true, spiritual magic. The focusing of one's mind and the directing of one's will are essential, but ultimately, the truly magical ingredients are you and your connection to the Divine."

"God is like a giant, glittering diamond; each facet on that diamond is the belief system of a positive religion," RavenWolf says. And, as all witches know, there's magic in believing.

How Witches Perform Magick

Lady Sabrina

Magick gives witches the ability to control events. However, the witch's strength of character and mental ability have much to do with how well magick works. Four basic principles form the cornerstone of effective magick: knowledge, will or desire, courage, and silence. In order to bring about change, the magickal process depends on the witch's creative visualization of the change, belief that he or she possesses the power to make the change, and the desire to make the change. A witch must truly believe in magick for the spells and incantations to work. Lady Sabrina is a high priestess and founder of Our Lady of Enchantment Seminary of Wicca. Based in Nashua, New Hampshire, Our Lady of Enchantment is the world's largest school of Wicca and magick. She is also the author of several books, including *Secrets of Modern Witchcraft Revealed* and *Exploring Wicca*.

Excerpted from *Exploring Wicca: The Beliefs, Rites, and Rituals of the Wiccan Religion*, by Lady Sabrina (Franklin Lakes, NJ: New Page Books, 2000). Copyright © 2000 by Lady Sabrina. Reprinted with permission.

"Magick is the art of making changes in reality by acts of Will and Imagination. Magick could be said to be the Art, encompassing all other arts; it is a way of creating the world."
—Bill Whitcomb, *The Magician's Companion*

Witchcraft is the celebration of life, and magick is the ability to control it. Magick is the one thing that can really help improve life, is something everyone can do, and is only as good or evil as the person using it. Magick is a science that brings those who practice it into alignment with the natural forces of the universe. By using the powers of the mind, in combination with certain objects, the magician manipulates the forces of the universe to bend or change reality according to his or her own will.

Magick, like any philosophy, has infinite possibilities, as well as distinct limitations. It relies heavily on the strength of character and mental ability of the individual using it. Magick also depends on belief much more than it does on intent. What you really, truly believe is what will come into being—not what you simply want. If you don't believe in what you are doing, then all the spells, candles, and incantations in the world will not work.

The Principles of Magick

As a science, magick has certain principles that are at the heart of its mechanics. The first principle is the Principle of Similarity. The second is the Principle of Contact or Contagion. Both of these principles come under the designation of Sympathetic Magick.

The Principle of Similarity is also referred to as Homeopathic or Imitative Magick. It states that like produces like, or that an effect may resemble its cause. Simply put, whatever you do to the symbolic representation of a person, place, or thing will directly affect that same person, place, or thing.

A good example of homeopathic magick is the Voodoo

doll, created by practitioners when they wish to influence someone. The doll is fashioned to look like the person they wish to influence. Then, depending upon the circumstances, the practitioners will proceed to heal or hurt their targeted victims through magickal conjurations. Because the dolls look like (imitate) the intended victims, they are capable of creating a link with them. The intentions of the practitioner then travel through the link, impacting what is at the other end.

In partnership with the principle of Similarity is the principle of Contact or Contagion. This principle states that things that have been in contact with each other will continue to act on each other, even at a distance, after all physical contact has been broken. Because of this, it is possible to use a person's picture, clothing, or handwriting as a magickal link. These links are often referred to as "lag-locks" or "relics," and are of primary importance in certain spells and enchantments, especially when love and friendship are involved. As in homeopathic magick, what is done to the link will create an effect on the intended target.

The Four Cornerstones of Magick

In addition to the principles of Similarity and Contagion, most practitioners adhere to the four cornerstones of magick. These four principles are expressed in the ability *to know, to will, to dare,* and *to keep silent.*

1. *To Know.* This refers to knowledge about magick and what makes it work. The practitioner must know and understand the basic working principles of a magickal operation before he or she attempts it. There is a saying in magick that knowledge is power, so if the practitioner wants power, then he or she must first have knowledge.

2. *To Will.* This is the ability to concentrate, focus attention, and direct the will to manifest desire. Practitioners

must be able to force their will upon the universe, in a positive and powerful way, to accomplish their desires. In magick, practitioners must be able to control their surroundings, which include the mind and body.

3. *To Dare*. This is the courage to challenge ideas. Magicians must be able to stand up for what they believe in and be able to demand their rights. They must dare to have the courage to make their will manifest desire, without fear or doubt. The magician must be able to command respect from his or her peers, as well as from the forces with which they work. They must dare to be strong.

4. *To Keep Silent*. This is by far the hardest of the four rules. The practitioner must shut out, and off, all outside distractions and learn to concentrate and focus. Silence also has a partner, the mouth. The well-trained magician knows how to keep it shut and not crow about every little thing she does. This is because every time she speaks of the magickal works she is doing, she dissipates her energy and power. This is why you don't hear Witches and magicians bragging about what they did or are doing.

The Magickal Process

Creative Visualization. One of the most important aspects of any magickal work is creative visualization. It is considered to be the key to success and personal power. Creative visualization is a process or technique used for making dreams and wishes come true. In essence, creative visualization is a fancy name for the old children's game of "let's pretend."

The magician creates an image in his or her mind of a person, place, or thing that he or she desires to have or to affect. This image is then empowered through magickal incantations and then acted upon during ritual. The psychic energy directed toward the mind image causes it to physically manifest.

There are three guidelines, comparable to the Witch's Pyramid, that the magician follows when using creative visualization. These guidelines, belief, desire, and visualization, are referred to as the *Witch's Mystical Triangle.*

The Witch's Mystical Triangle

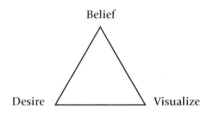

Guideline One: Belief. This is a very important guideline. Practitioners must believe in their goals or objects of desire if they are going to achieve them. There is a saying that what you believe can happen, you can make happen. Witches and magicians know they must have faith. They must believe in their personal power if they are going to get anywhere in magick or life.

Guideline Two: Desire. There must be a strong desire. You won't see competent Witches or magicians sitting around wishing for this or that. If there is something they need or desire, they use their powers to get it. They will be obsessed with their goal. This obsession stirs their emotions into action and gives them the power to achieve.

Guideline Three: Visualize. This is the most important guideline of all. Practitioners must be able to create a clear mental picture or duplicate image of their desires in their minds. They must be able to see the thing they desire, just as if they were looking at a photograph. Being able to actually see, within the mind, what they want is the key to making it manifest.

Practicing Witches or magicians will take photographs,

draw, and even visit and/or touch the object of their desire. Then, within the bounds of the magick circle, they will recreate mentally what they desire. Through willpower and focused energy they visualize their desire into reality. . . .

Magick is an art and a science. It gives you the ability to make changes in your life. Through creative visualization and the movement of energy, you are able to manipulate the forces of nature to recreate your reality. Consider magick high-powered, positive thinking that can give you the upper hand in life. Remember: What the mind can imagine, the will can create.

Harry Potter Books Are a Good Reading Choice for Youth

Michael G. Maudlin

Some Christians have expressed concern that the Harry Potter series of books expose children to a world of witchcraft and moral relativism. While well-meaning, some of these critics overstate the dangers of the series. The books are fun entertainment, and Harry Potter himself is a good youth who just happens to be a wizard. The books are full of courage, loyalty, compassion, joy, and even humility—all admirable virtues. Good and evil are clear and absolute in the books, and readers will learn little about the true world of the occult. Michael G. Maudlin is the online executive editor of *Christianity Today*.

I was one of two "religious" representatives on a panel about "Morality at the Movies." The diverse route included

From "Virtue on a Broomstick," by Michael G. Maudlin, *Christianity Today*, September 4, 2000. Copyright © 2000 by Christianity Today, Inc. Reprinted with permission.

movie industry people, journalists, and lawyers, but somehow I got branded as the radical. Here is what I proposed: parents should support one another as they try to guide their kids on which movies are appropriate to see. "My kids know much better than I do which movies are best for them," one parent responded. "What right do parents have to say what is right for teenagers?" said one college student. "What's the big deal?" another adult chimed in. "As long as it doesn't support hate and violence, it's just entertainment."

The discussion soon became heated and enjoyable, but I came away surprised at the cultural resistance to adults' acting like parents. Even in this post-Columbine era, daring to say which entertainment choices ennoble and which degrade children gets one quickly branded a "fundamentalist."

So I have read the CHRISTIANS OBJECT TO HARRY POTTER headlines with a jaundiced eye. These Christian protesters are newsworthy only because in our culture there is so little debate about what is good for our kids. Christians often serve as the cultural superego. In a morally chaotic world, it has become our task to voice objections to moral deviance, and it is the mainstream culture's job to tell us why we are "uptight," "ridiculous," and/or "bigoted." Along comes a popular children series about witchcraft and journalists scurry to their Rolodexes, looking under "F" for "frothy fundamentalists" to get a good quote. Thus when a relatively small number of Christian parents ask that their kids' schools not read Harry Potter, we read about it in all the major newspapers.

Bewitched

At 12:01 A.M. on July 7, 2000, Pottermania struck again with the release of book four in the series, *Harry Potter and the Goblet of Fire*. With a recordbreaking first printing of 3.5 million in the United States, the book caused long lines of eager fans. . . . Among those line–dwellers were many evangelicals.

In fact, I would guess that the vast majority of evangelicals in this country who have encountered Harry Potter are as smitten with him as the culture at large. Many of my Christian friends bragged to me about their late-night family outing to purchase the book (I waited for the free review copy) and were eager to compare notes on whether the latest volume matched the quality of the first three.

Much has been written about evangelicals' engagement with the culture and our drive to shore up crumbling family values via a Judeo-Christian ethic. And it is this impulse that warms the hearts of so many evangelicals when we read Rowling. The Harry Potter series is not only laugh-out-loud fun, but Harry is good.

For those out of the loop, Harry is the orphaned son of two loving parents (albeit a witch and a wizard) who were murdered by one of the best embodiments of evil in fiction that has come along in some time, Lord Voldemort (watch out Nicolae Carpathia!)—or as most of the characters in the books call him, "He-who-must-not-be-named."

The one-year-old Harry is mysteriously spared from being killed because of "the sacrificial love" of his mother, and Voldemort comes perilously close to dying when his spell against Harry backfires. The lightning-bolt scar on his forehead and the eternal enmity of Voldemort are all that Harry takes away from the struggle.

Raised by his Muggle (nonmagical) uncle and aunt, the Dursleys, who hate all things magical, Harry suffers through a Dickensian childhood of sleeping in the cupboard under the stairs and never receiving a birthday present, all the while watching his same-aged cousin Dudley being spoiled with food and presents galore. All this changes when Harry turns 11 and discovers he is a wizard, famous in the magical world for defeating Voldemort, and attends boarding school at Hogwarts School of Witchcraft and Wizardry. (The Dursleys tell their friends that Harry is at St. Brutus's Secure Center for Incurably Criminal Boys). Each volume covers a year in Harry's life at Hogwarts, where with his best friends Ron and Hermione he struggles against a plot to do him in amid his school and extracurricular activities.

Now for year four. The consensus is that *Goblet of Fire* is not only twice as long as any of the others but also better. The orphaned English wizard is now 14 and ready for more responsibility. It comes when he is illegally entered in the Triwizard Tournament (he is technically too young to participate). Harry knows that someone entered him in order to do him harm, but everyone thinks he rigged the ballot for his own glory. Thus our hero suffers ostracism from his friends, even Ron, while figuring out how to survive the tournament. And how does Harry cope? Yes, he gets discouraged and angry, but overall he displays courage, loyalty, compassion, joy, humility, even love. During the tournament, Harry must choose between winning and ensuring that others remain free from danger; he chooses the latter while hardly batting an eye. And all the while he sounds like a typical 14-year-old. That is Rowling's triumph: creating a "cool" good kid.

Dark Magic

What are Christians actually complaining about when they critique Rowling? Far from frothing at the mouth, many Christian leaders have given reasoned counsel on the matter.

Lindy Beam, a youth-culture analyst for *Plugged In*, a Focus on the Family newsletter that reviews popular culture, has surveyed the Potter phenomenon and provides helpful guidance for parents. She begins by stating what should be the obvious goal for parents today but is not: "To grow kids who are wise, thoughtful, culturally literate, pure, God-fearing, and who can make a positive impact on their world."

Next she raises three issues Christian parents should grapple with before they allow Harry Potter into their child's imagination: First, the series may desensitize us to witchcraft. Second, the books don't "acknowledge any supernatural powers or moral authority at all." And third, there is "lots of gore and fright." But then she lists the books' positive values and cautions against overreaction. "Children who read about Harry will probably discover little to nothing about the true world of the occult," she writes. "We know God hates the practice of witchcraft (Deut. 18:10). But we have committed a fault of logic in saying that reading about witches and wizards necessarily translates into these occult practices. I would propose instead that reading Harry Potter produces curiosity and that it is what we do with that curiosity that makes all the difference."

John Andrew Murray, Beam's colleague at Teachers in Focus, has harsher words for Harry: "By disassociating magic and supernatural evil, it becomes possible to portray occult practices as 'good' and 'healthy,' contrary to the scriptural declaration that such practices are 'detestable to the Lord.' This, in turn, opens the door for kids to become fascinated with the supernatural while tragically failing to seek or recognize the one true source of supernatural good—namely God."

"What comes across," Murray concludes, "is a kind of dualism, the idea that there are two equal, untreated, antagonistic forces, one good and one evil, and that choosing between the two is purely a matter of personal opinion. Rowling's readers are ultimately left in a morally confused world."

I disagree with Murray. I think good and evil are clear and absolute in the books, just not fully explained—yet. It may be your "personal opinion" that it is right to serve Lord Voldemort, but every reader knows which side you have chosen. And I would shout a little more loudly the wonderful virtues that are modeled in the books, which is why Charles Colson and Fuller Seminary president Richard Mouw have reviewed the books positively.

Still, none of the critics sounds like a simplistic book-burner to me. We may disagree on details, but we share the same concern in taking seriously our charge to raise morally and religiously informed children. Overall I think the Christian community can feel proud of how it has mobilized itself regarding Harry.

To be sure, the ending is scary, which often happens when one tries to portray true evil, and so several reviewers suggest the books be limited to children ten and older, which sounds right to me. Yet as the book closes, Harry's future looks promising and intriguing: Harry has grown up and become a true player in the moral battle of his time, in a world where many witches and wizards do not want to admit there is a war.

For Christian readers, this and other themes in this non-Christian book will seem appropriate for the world they find themselves engaged with.

Wiccans Must Be Permitted to Serve in the U.S. Military

Ontario Consultants on Religious Tolerance

Christian groups have objected to allowing Wiccans to serve in the U.S. military. However, Wicca has been recognized as a valid religion since as early as 1988 and has been active in the United States since the 1950s. Wiccans on military bases have not been granted special privileges; it is the main-stream religions that have benefits—such as chaplains, on-base meeting halls, and office support—that are not available to Wiccans. Concerns about the effects of allowing Wiccans in the military are unfounded. Wiccans will not undermine the readiness or functioning of the armed forces. The Ontario Consultants on Religious Tolerance is an organization that provides accurate information about minority religions, cults, and sects and attempts to expose religious fraud and misinformation.

From "Wiccans and Military Preparedness," by Ontario Consultants on Religious Tolerance, www.religioustolerance.org, August 27, 2001. Copyright © 2001 by Ontario Consultants on Religious Tolerance. Reprinted with permission.

Lt. Col. Robert L. Maginnis (U.S. Army, Ret.) has written a paper for the conservative Christian group, the Family Research Council (FRC).[1,2] He is the director of their Military Readiness Project. The paper seems to have been triggered by a boycott of some conservative Christian groups against the U.S. Army.

The FRC was initially organized by Focus on the Family, another conservative Christian organization, under the leadership of Gary Bauer, a candidate for the presidency of the U.S. in the year 2000.

The conclusion of the paper is that the *"Pentagon should withdraw recognition of Wicca for readiness reasons."* Maginnis feels that certain religious rights of Wiccans in the army should be terminated, because Wiccans are a threat to unit cohesion, morale, and efficiency in the Army.

The following is our interpretation of Maginnis' paper. You should read the entire text of his paper to get the full flavor of his objections.[1] Maginnis raised the following points:

Wicca Is a Valid Religion

He recognizes that Wicca has been formally recognized as a valid religion by the Army since 1996. He did mention that many Wiccan groups have been given tax exempt status. Unfortunately he did not mention that:

• The Army actually recognized Wicca much earlier. Since 1990, its chaplains' guide which deals with minority religions, has included Wicca.

• Various U.S. courts have also recognized Wicca as a valid religion (e.g., a 1988 decision by a U.S. district court).

He is concerned that, because of the recognition of Wicca, that *"any fringe religion will now have to be granted special benefits by DOD [Department of Defense]."* This statement concerns a number of errors:

• Wicca is not a fringe religion. It has been active in the U.S. for about 5 decades. Wiccans have taken part in many inter-faith conferences, such as the World's Parliament of Religions. They have about 200,000 members in the U.S.

• Each religion that asks to be recognized by the U.S. military is not automatically accepted. Religions are considered on their own merits, and must meet military requirements. For example, the Wiccans at Ft. Hood, TX, had to agree to requirements governing ritual clothing and restrictions on the use of their ritual athames before they were accepted by the DOD.

• Wiccans and other minority religions have not been *"granted special benefits."* They have merely been allowed to use base facilities for their rituals. It is the larger religions which have been granted special privileges. For example, the military hires chaplains, provides office support, and usually provides an on-base religious meeting place for its Christian, Jewish and often Muslim soldiers.

Even if the DOD spent the hundreds of thousands of dollars necessary to hire Wiccan priests and priestesses to act as army chaplains, the Army would not be giving special privileges to Wiccans; they would only be giving the standard privileges that Christians, Jews and Muslims have enjoyed for years.

Concern over Military Readiness

He is concerned that if the Army allows Wiccans to hold their services on-base, then non-Wiccan soldiers' *"readiness factors such as military values, adherence to norms, willingness to kill, and recruitment and retention . . ."* will be undermined. This is because he believes that most soldiers regard *"witchcraft as an abomination."*

• *Diversity:* It is quite possible to maintain an army that is totally male, totally white, totally heterosexual and totally monotheistic. However, in its wisdom, the U.S. army became integrated a few decades ago; they have allowed women into an increasing range of assignments. They do not reject those gays and lesbians who stay in the closet. Finally, they are now formally recognizing small minority religions. At each step of the way, doomsayers raised the specter of damaged military preparedness. History has shown their concerns to be without merit. As armies are increasingly directed at peace keeping, a force that is racially, sexually and religiously diverse sends a powerful message to the people being helped. Kosovo and Bosnia are two potent examples of the power of religious diversity in the military.

- *Monotheism:* Maginnis apparently wants to add a new religious requirement for joining the U.S. army: the belief in monotheism.
  - But Muslims and Jews are the only large religions in U.S. society that are totally monotheistic.
  - Christians are generally trinitarian—they believe in a Father, Son and Holy Spirit. Some even have a pantheon of supernatural entities to whom their members pray, including the Trinity, supported by hundreds of saints.
  - Many Wiccans are in fact monotheists. They believe in the existence of a single deity that is unknowable and remote. They then recognize and interact with two aspects of this single deity: a female Goddess and a male God.
- *Religious intolerance:* He implies that religious intolerance by Christians and Jews towards Wiccans is a valid reason for eliminating Wiccans from the armed forces.
  - There remains even today in the armed forces some racial bigotry. But the DOD chooses to fight this by teaching and requiring tolerance, rather than allowing discrimination against minority races.
  - Some degree of sexism remains. Again, the DOD teaches tolerance rather than expel female soldiers.

• There will always be religious bigotry intolerance and hatred. But the DOD is teaching acceptance. Their only other option is to expel, or limit the religious rights, of followers of minority religions. And this is clearly unconstitutional.

Confusing Wicca and Witchcraft

He implies that Wicca is not only un-Christian and un-Judaic, but is a *"direct affront"* to those religions. He links Wicca in America with condemnations of "Witchcraft" and "Sorcery" in the Bible.

• Even if modern-day Wicca were similar to the practices translated as "Witchcraft" and "Sorcery" in some English translations of the Bible, the 1st Amendment to the U.S. Constitution requires that the government and its agencies not discriminate against religious groups.

• Although various English translations of the Bible do condemn Witchcraft, these references clearly have nothing to do with Wicca:

  • The term "Wiccan" is well defined. It refers to a follower of a NeoPagan religion, who is specifically required to follow the Wiccan Rede and do no harm to others. "Witch" and "Witchcraft" have so many mutually conflicting meanings that they should never be used in essays, reports—and particularly in English translations of the Bible

  • In order to understand what the Exodus 22:18 and Deuteronomy 18:10–11 really mean, it is necessary to consult the original Hebrew. The passages condemn m'khaseph who are evil sorcerers using spoken spells to harm others. Wiccans are specifically prohibited from hurting others by their Wiccan Rede. Similarly Galatians 5:19 is often translated as condemning sorcery and/or witchcraft. The original Greek word here is pharmakia from which the English word "pharmacy" is derived. It refers to the practice of preparing poisonous potions to harm or kill others. Again, Wiccans are prohibited from following this or any other practices that harms people. The Bible clearly condemns evil sorcerers, not benign Wiccans.

• Maginnis writes that *"Witchcraft, also known as Wicca, the craft, or the craft of the wise, is a religion."* He is correct in stating that Wicca is often called *"the craft,"* and *"the craft of the wise."* But "Witchcraft" is in no way a synonym for "Wicca." The terms "Witch" and "Witchcraft" have been used to refer to African native healers, evil sorcerers, Satanists, very beautiful women, very ugly women, a person who searches for water, a follower of syncretistic Caribbean religions such as Santeria, Vodun, a male magician, a wife who is not submissive to her husband, and an expert in their field. Many Wiccans avoid associating the term "Witchcraft" with their religion because of the mass confusion that it causes. Others wish to retain the term because to abandon it would be disrespectful for the innocent people slaughtered by the Christian church during the Burning Times. We feel that writers should avoid the term, unless they wish to project hatred, misunderstanding and intolerance.

• The phrase: *"A witch holds pagan beliefs, but not all pagans are witches"* is, by itself, meaningless. That is because the term "witch" has so many mutually contradictory meanings. The statement *"A Wiccan holds Neopagan beliefs, but not all Neopagans are Wiccans"* is valid.

• Maginnis makes the common Christian error of equating Wicca with Druidism and other Neopagan religions. The term "Neopagan" describes a class of religions; it is similar to the term "Eastern religions." Within Neopaganism is a number of different religions, including Asatru, Druidism, and Wicca. Within Wicca are a number of traditions, which resemble the denominations of Christianity.

Background of Wicca

Maginnis correctly describes the origin and some of the basic beliefs of Wiccans. Wiccans do stress the importance of the feminine in society. Most are accepting of persons of all sexual orientations. Many feminists have indeed been attracted to Wicca because it lacks the patriarchal beliefs of most monotheistic religions.

He quotes Probe Ministries, a counter-cult group which is opposed to new or small religious movements which differ from historical Christianity. They state: *"The rise of the goddess is a direct assault on the patriarchal foundation of Christianity."* Probe Ministries seems to confuse religions which are *un*-Christian with religions that are *anti*-Christian. Most Wiccans view women and men as equals. This is unlike the status of women as described in much of the Bible. However, Wicca is no more of an *"assault on . . . Christianity"* than are liberal and mainline Christians, who also have non-sexist policies and beliefs.

Concerns over Pacifism

Wiccans who wish to join the armed forces must come to terms with their main rule of behavior: the Wiccan Rede *"An ye harm none, do what ye will"* (in modern English, *"do whatever you wish, as long as it does not harm anybody including yourself"*). Picking up an assault rifle, charging an enemy position, and trying to kill everyone there certainly does harm to others.

However, Wiccans are not unique in this problem. All but a very few religions teach an ethic of reciprocity that prohibits harming or killing others. In Christianity, this is called the Golden Rule. A few examples are:

- Baha'i: *"And if thine eyes be turned towards justice, choose thou for thy neighbour that which thou choosest for thyself."*
- Christianity: *"Therefore all things whatsoever ye would that men should do to you, do ye even so to them."*
- Buddhism: *"Hurt not others in ways that you yourself would find hurtful."*
- Islam: *"Not one of you is a believer until he loves for his brother what he loves for himself."*
- Judaism & Christianity: *". . . thou shalt love thy neighbor as thyself."*
- Native American Spirituality: *"Respect for all life is the foundation."*

Followers of all of these religions who wish to enter the army must decide how to handle their faith's teaching to not harm others. In fact, Christians have an additional hurdle not shared by Wiccans: one of the Ten Commandments. Exodus 20:13 specifically says *"Thou shalt not kill."* (KJV) Most individuals come to terms with their faith by citing self-defense and protecting one's country as considerations which override their religion's teachings. Others simply avoid joining the armed forces. During warfare, many Quakers (members of the Society of Friends) and others became conscientious objectors.

One might assume that all applicants to the armed forces have come to terms with this religious conflict. Wiccans in no way differ from followers of other religions on this matter. Pacifism within Wicca is not a concern to the army.

His references to Isaac Bonewits and the Arn Draiocht Fein (ADF) are not particularly meaningful, because Bonewits is a Druid. Druidism is a different religion from Wicca.

Concerns over Ethical Relativism

Maginnis quotes The Covenant of the Goddess as saying *"[W]hat is good for one may be evil for another and vice versa."*[3]

This, of course, is merely a reflection of ethical diversity within American society. Some people believe that wives should be submissive to their husbands and that equal power sharing in marriage is forbidden; others believe the opposite. Some believe that an early abortion is the least unethical action for a woman in some circumstances; others believe that abortion involves the murder of a human being. The list goes on endlessly.

He quotes the Circle Sanctuary's web site that says: *"Witches have no specific taboos against speaking any particular words, consensual sexual acts among individuals capable of rational consent, or breaking laws they know to be unjust."*[4] This statement is generally true:

• Wiccans have no reserved words that must not be spoken, like the name of G-d in Judaism. Christianity does not have reserved words either.

• Wiccans do not generally object to consensual sexual acts between mature people, particularly if they are done within a committed, dedicated, monogamous relationship. They typically condemn sexual activity between individuals where manipulation, coercion, force, or undue influence are involved. But religious liberals, many religious moderates, and the laws in most of North America agree with this stance.

• Rarely, Wiccans will knowingly break laws that they know to be unjust or unconstitutional. Some held a demonstration in North Carolina against an obviously unconstitutional state law which prohibits reading of palms, use of tarot cards, casting runes, etc.—whether for money, done as an amateur, or done alone in the privacy of one's home. Quiet protest against unethical laws is an established American practice for those brave souls who are willing to accept the consequences. Faced with a constitution that guarantees personal religious freedom and a state law that eliminates that freedom, some Wiccans will willingly break the unjust law in order to be charged and have the law declared unconstitutional.

Concerns over Wiccan Magical Practices

Magic is definitely part of some witches' religious practice:

• Most Wiccans do cast spells. But they are normally prohibited unless they are done with the prior consent of the recipient of the spell. And they are never done if the spell is manipulative, coercive or may harm anyone. Love spells which are designed to influence a person to fall in love with another individual are not allowed. These are not particularly different from a Christian's blessing and prayer.

• Some forms of sex magic involve actual sexual activities. These are occasionally performed by some Wiccans. However, the ritual is done in private by a couple who are in a committed relationship.

• Some witches *"believe that the dead join the Blessed Ancestors, who watch over, protect and advise their descendants."*[3] This is very similar to some Christians who pray for support and guidance from dead saints.

• There is no *"basic Wiccan dedication ritual"* as stated in Maginnis' paper. Different Wiccan traditions have various rituals for dedication and initiation. There are probably thousands of them in existence.

Concerns over Military Readiness

Maginnis cites a number of concerns about the adverse effect that Wiccans would have over military readiness. None seem to be valid:

• Wiccans are *"noted for their ethical relativism."* This is common among all Neopagans, religious liberals and religious moderates. It results in a person carefully considering their decisions—an advantage in today's army.

• Wiccans approve of consensual acts by persons of minority sexual orientation. This is probably true, although we are unaware of any surveys that would confirm that. This is also the policy of the DOD ever since they implemented their *"don't ask, don't tell"* guidelines. Thus, all soldiers are required to support this policy.

• Wiccans in the armed forces are not pacifists. If they were pacifists then, like most Quakers, they never would have joined the army. Wiccans in the army have come to terms with the Wiccan Rede, just as the majority Christians have come to terms with their Golden Rule and 10 commandments.

• All that Wiccans have asked for is to be allowed to practice their religion like the Christians, Jews and Muslims. They do not ask for special religious facilities; they do not ask for professional chaplains. In fact, if the majority of soldiers were Wiccans, the armed forces' task of providing for the spiritual need of its soldiers would be significantly simplified. There would be no need for chaplains and supporting facilities. All Wiccans ask for is access to existing rooms and permission to hold their rituals on the base.

• It is true that many English versions of the Bible label *"witchcraft as an abomination."* Eating cheeseburgers or wearing shirts made of polyester-cotton blends is also an abomination, according to the Bible. But the Bible's original Hebrew and Greek do not mention Wicca. The words mistranslated as "Witch" and "Witchcraft" are totally unrelated to Wiccans and Wicca.

• Many conservative Christians believe that the Bible is inerrant. The New Testament contains passages that state that the Gods and Goddesses of non-Judeo-Christians are really Satan or his demons. Since conservative Christian soldiers have to accept what they regard as Satan worshipers in their midst, there should be no difficulty for them to accept Wiccans.

• The Army has stated that Wiccans do not represent a discipline problem or adversely affect military readiness.

For many decades, the armed forces have made major contributions towards diminishing internal hatred, bigotry and intolerance. Society has benefited greatly from these policies. Decades ago, they racially integrated the military. Over the past decade, they have greatly reduced sexism in the military by allowing women to accept an increasing range of combat positions. Recently they have learned to accept persons with minority sexual orientations, as long as they *"don't tell."* And now, they are formally recognizing small minority religions. The result is an armed forces that fully reflects the diversity of American culture. This will become increasingly important in the future, as military roles evolve.

Positive Aspects of Maginnis' Paper

Lt. Col. Robert L. Maginnis' paper contained a number of positive items that are infrequently found in Christian essays:

• He capitalized references to Wicca and Wiccans. This is a small item, but an encouraging one. Although most writers capitalize the names of religions and their followers (e.g., Christianity, Christian) out of respect, many Christian web sites omit this when referring to Neopagan religions.

• He mentioned bisexuality as a sexual behavior. Most conservative Christian websites basically recognize only one sexual orientation: heterosexuality. Homosexuality is usually described as an addiction or a deviate behavior, rather than as an orientation. Bisexuality is rarely mentioned at all.

• Perhaps the main encouraging sign in Maginnis' paper is that he consulted Neopagan sources to find descriptions of Wiccan beliefs and practices. He describes Wicca fairly accurately. He does not describe them as evil people, murderers who barbeque babies for breakfast, abortion providers who consider abortion to be a religious ritual, etc., as in so many other Christian web sites. For decades, conservative Christians have written books, given lectures, and (recently) created web sites attacking Wiccans as profoundly evil people. They have based almost all of their writings, directly or indirectly, on Christian propaganda from the 15th to 18th centuries. These were the burning times when the church was actively exterminating what it regarded as heretics. For what we believe is the first time, Wiccans are being criticized on a conservative Christian website for being too gentle and nice, not willing to kill other human beings. Maginnis' paper will be a useful essay for Wiccans to use as a reference when they are trying to convince conservative Christians that they are not kidnappers, torturers, and murderers of children, or Satan worshipers.

Notes

1. R.L. Maginnis, "Brewing up trouble: Wicca and the U.S. Military," Family Research Council, at: http://www.frc.org/papers/milred.

2. Printed copies of the essay can be requested from the Family Research Council at (800) 225-4008. This is a toll-free number accessible from the U.S. and Canada.

3. "Witchcraft: Commonly-Asked Questions, Straightforward Answers," Covenant of the Goddess, at: http://www.cog.org/wicca/faq.html.

4. "Circle Sanctuary—A Pledge to Pagan Spirituality," at: http://www.circlesanctuary.org/contact/PSApledge.html.

Epilogue: Analyzing the Evidence

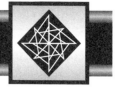

Witches and their magical arts have endured for thousands of years. Indeed, some modern witches claim that the earliest witches were healers who used their knowledge and power to treat those in need more than fifty thousand years ago. During a time when nothing was known about what caused disease or illness, witches—who were known for their medical wisdom—were the one hope people had to treat and cure medical problems. While some witches worked exclusively as healers, others expanded their repertoire to include magic performed to ensure good hunting and favorable weather for crops, to protect the health of farm animals, to foretell the future, and to communicate with the dead.

Magical Tools

Witches were extremely knowledgeable about the different properties of plants. They had to be to know that thorn apple, nightshade, monkshood, hemlock, and cinquefoil had hallucinogenic properties, and according to some, gave them the ability to fly, at least in their minds. Witches used periwinkle, poppies, mandrake, endive, and roses in potions for love and other magical spells. Staples in the healer's garden included foxglove, ground ivy, vervain, wild celery, and parsley, plants that were effective for treating everything from heart disease to muscle cramps to labor pains to inducing abortion.

Science has determined that many of these plants do

have invaluable properties for treating many medical conditions. But in the early days of witchcraft, few people could read and even fewer knew anything about science or medicine. Thus, to an ignorant peasant, someone who used common plants to cure sickness or stop pain seemed to have truly magical powers. Moreover, given the widespread belief in magic, it is easy to conclude that some potions worked merely because the patient believed they would, a phenomenon that doctors today call the placebo effect.

Despite their healing abilities, witches were feared by their neighbors. Many people believed that if witches had the power to heal, then surely they had the power to cause harm as well. Since nothing was known about the causes and transmission of illnesses and diseases, if well water became poisoned or a baby died during childbirth, it was often blamed on witchcraft. People readily believed that a person who used magic to help those in need would also use magic to harm those she disliked.

The Rise of Christianity

Through much of its history, Christianity has acknowledged the presence and power of witches. For the first several hundred years after its founding, the church coexisted peacefully with witches. But as the church gained strength and influence during the Dark Ages, the pagan beliefs of witches threatened Christianity. Church leaders were no longer willing to turn a blind eye to pantheistic and polytheistic beliefs. The church began to demonize witchcraft and other pagan faiths; it claimed that witches were evil beings who worked with the devil and that the gods and goddesses that witches worshiped were actually satanic and, therefore, enemies of God and the church. A council of bishops warned Louis the Pious of the Holy Roman Empire in 829 about the dangers of witches:

> Their *malefica* [wickedness] can disturb the air, bring down
> hail, foretell the future, remove the fruits and milk from one
> person and give them to another, and perform innumerable
> marvels. . . . Their overweening audacity does not shrink
> from serving the Devil.[1]

Church leaders used witchcraft as a convenient scapegoat
for the existence of evil in the world. New converts (and
dedicated Christians as well) often questioned how God
could permit evil and wickedness if he was omnipotent and
loving. In the fifth century, Saint Augustine of Hippo tried
to answer that question. He wrote that God had created two
worlds: one populated by angels and morally upright
people and the other inhabited by demons, pagans, and
other agents of the devil. The devil's army was continually
trying to steal Christian souls, he wrote, and it used magic,
sorcery, witchcraft, and other tools to do so. Therefore,
church leaders decreed, even well-intentioned spells and
charms, such as those that were meant to help heal the sick,
were instruments of the devil and were, therefore, forbidden. Folk healers were now relegated to the same evil status
as witches, soothsayers, and other demons.

Underlying the church's opposition to magic, witchcraft,
and sorcery was the belief that a witch entered into a con-
tract with the devil. In exchange for the witch's soul, the
devil granted the witch supernatural powers and all her
worldly desires, such as wealth, a husband (or, in the case
of male witches, a wife), security, or material possessions.
This contention became such an article of faith that it lasted
well into the seventeenth century. A transcript of the Salem
witch trials notes, for example, that the devil needed the
support and allegiance of witches to "over Come the Kingdome of Christ, and set up [his own] Kingdome."[2]

More fundamental still to the church's position was that,
by definition, making a pact with the devil required witches

to repudiate Christianity. This was done in multiple steps, the first of which was the desecration of the ultimate symbol of Christianity—the cross. According to *Compendium Maleficarum* (*Handbook of Witches*) written in 1626, witches were also "rebaptized in the name of the Devil, and having renounced his Christian name, takes another." Then they swore allegiance to their new leader in a sacred circle drawn on the ground. Next, the handbook's authors note, "the witches request the Devil that their names be struck out of the book of life and inscribed in the book of death." (It was at this time that the devil supposedly placed his mark on the witch. The mark—a wart, mole, birthmark, extra nipple, or other blemish—identified the witch as one of the devil's servants.) The handbook notes that witches were also required to sacrifice children to the devil, "killing one by sorcery every month or sucking its blood every fortnight." Finally, the pact is sealed when the witches swore before an enthroned devil that all Christian symbols would be treated as profane and that they would "maintain the strictest silence about their traffic with the devil."[3]

Many accused witches admitted their transgressions to judges and juries. Some of these confessions were freely given, others were not. Tituba, a slave originally from Barbados, denied—despite trick questions during her pretrial examination for witchcraft in Salem in 1692—that she had any familiarity with evil spirits. Finally, however, tired and unable to withstand the hostile and unrelenting interrogation, Tituba decided to tell the court what it wanted to hear. She "confessed" that she had seen the devil, who appeared to her as a man the night before. In response to questions, Tituba gave detailed answers about the evil deeds the devil expected her to perform (all the while protesting her innocence); the pretty rewards, such as a yellow bird, he offered her in return; and the sabbats she had attended by riding on a broomstick with Sarah Osborne and Sarah Good sitting behind her.

Many other so-called confessions were offered under torture. In Germany, where a witch was required to confess before she could be executed, the torture usually began with thumbscrews, followed by a whipping, and then vises that squeezed and broke the leg and ankle bones. If a witch still refused to confess, a period on the rack was next. Clara Geissler, a sixty-nine-year-old German widow accused of witchcraft, admitted on the rack that she had stolen sixty babies, murdered them, and then drank their blood. When she was released from the rack, she immediately recanted her confession; she was tortured a second time until she confessed again. She recanted once again, only to be tortured a third time. She died during this third period of torture, but the report documenting her confessions claimed that "The Devil would not let her reveal anything more and so wrung her neck."[4]

The tortures that elicited confessions of consorting with the devil also brought shocking testimony regarding the sexual aspects of witchcraft. It was believed that the devil used sex to seduce many women into witchcraft. And once a woman became a witch, she was sexually insatiable; she could transform herself into a succubus, a beautiful but evil demon who had sex with sleeping men. Bernard Peach, a witness called during the Salem witchcraft trial of Susanna Martin (who was sixty-seven years old at the time), claimed that Martin came

> in at the window and jumpt downe upon the flower [floor]. Shee was in her hood and scarf and the same dress that shee was in before at metting the same day. Being com in, shee was coming up toward this deponents face but turned back to his feet and took hold of them and drew up his body into a heap and Lay upon him about an hour and half or 2 hours, in all which taim this deponent could not stir nor speake.[5]

Witches had sex not only with sleeping men but with incubi (male demons) and the devil, as well as with their animal familiars.

Witches were said to take part in sexual orgies during their sabbats, quarterly meetings in which they worshiped the devil. Most of the information regarding the goings-on at sabbats comes from confessions accused witches gave under torture. Subjected to hideously painful torture, witches admitted to kissing the devil's backside and genitals (in whatever shape he assumed for the sabbat—man, cat, goat, toad, crow, or other animal), as well as having sex with whomever was at the sabbat regardless of the age, gender, or familial relationship of their partners.

Given the prudish attitudes toward sex, especially during the sixteenth and seventeenth centuries, licentious behavior on the part of any woman could lead to charges of witchcraft. Cotton Mather, a Puritan minister during the Salem witch trials, wrote in *The Wonders of the Invisible World* that a woman who was a "probable" witch led a "lewd and naughty kind of Life."[6] Many women convicted of witchcraft during the trials in Salem in 1692 had appeared before the courts previously under the charges of adultery or fornication. Even some of those convicted of witchcraft came to believe there was a connection: Margaret Lakes, before she was hanged in Dorchester, Massachusetts, is said to have admitted that God was justified in having her convicted as a witch because "she had when a single woman played the harlot, and being with Child used means to destroy the fruit of her body to conceal her sin and shame."[7]

Modern Witchcraft

Modern-day witches say that these early beliefs about sabbats and witches in general are completely erroneous. First and most important of all, witches claim that their guiding principle is to celebrate life and honor and revere nature. Silver RavenWolf, a witch and author of many books on witchcraft, writes, "WitchCraft is a nature based, life-affirming religion that follows a moral code and seeks to build harmony among people, and empower the self and others."[8] Author and witch Margot Adler describes the religion of Wicca revived by Gerald Gardner in England during the 1950s. It was, she wrote,

> a peaceful, happy nature religion. Witches met in covens, led by a priestess. They worshipped two principal deities, the god of forests and what lies beyond [the Horned God], and the great Triple Goddess of fertility and rebirth. They met in the nude in a nine-foot circle and raised power from their bodies through dancing and chanting and meditative techniques.[9]

Because the Horned God is portrayed as wearing antlers, many Christians equate him with the devil, who is popularly depicted as having horns. Wiccans, however, vehemently deny that they are devil worshipers. Raymond Buckland, a witch and author of numerous books on witchcraft, writes that charging witches with "devil worship" is

> ridiculous. The Devil is a purely Christian invention, there being no mention of him before the New Testament. . . . The Wica [sic], therefore, by virtue of being a pre-Christian religion, do not even believe in the Devil, let alone worship him![10]

RavenWolf agrees, adding, "We do not accept the concept of 'absolute evil,' nor do we worship any entity known as 'Satan' or 'the Devil' as defined by Christian tradition. We do not seek power through the suffering of others, nor do we accept the concept that personal benefits can only be derived by denial to another."[11]

In addition, witches assert that Wicca is a bona fide religion. Their claim is supported by the U.S. government, which officially recognizes Wicca as a religion. Although

Wicca does not have a hierarchy headed by a spiritual leader, it does require witches to accept as an article of faith the Wiccan Rede. This statement governs all aspects of witchcraft and the lives of those who claim to be witches:

> Bide the Wiccan laws ye must, in perfect love and perfect trust.
> Live and let live—fairly take and fairly give.
> Cast the Circle thrice about to keep the evil spirits out.
> To bind the spell every time, let the spell be spake in rhyme.
> Soft of eye and light of touch—speak ye little, listen much. . . .
> Mind the threefold law ye should—three times bad and three times good. . . .
> Eight words the Wiccan Rede fulfill, an [if] ye harm none, do what ye will.[12]

According to the Wiccan Rede, witches are prohibited from doing anything—magical or otherwise—that will harm anyone, including themselves. In case witches need further discouragement from practicing evil magic, the Rule of Three complements the Wiccan Rede:

> Ever mind the Rule of Three,
> Three times what thou givest returns to thee.
> This lesson well, thou must learn,
> Thee only gets what thou dost earn![13]

In other words, any spell a witch performs will come back to that individual threefold. If the witch performs a spell that harms someone, then harm will return threefold—either three separate times or an injury that is three times worse than was asked in the original charm. The same is true with a beneficial spell; it, too, will return threefold.

Wiccan Rituals

Modern witches contend that their eight main sabbats are nothing like those imagined by Christians in earlier times.

The sabbats are festivals to celebrate the changing of the seasons and to thank the Goddess and God for the blessings received during the year. Witches use the sabbats to celebrate and contemplate birth, life, death, and rebirth as seen in nature and the seasons. The most important sabbat is Samhein (pronounced Sow-en), on October 31. Samhein is the Wiccan New Year. Beltane, celebrated on April 30, marks the first half of the new year. Imbolc, held on February 1, and Lummas or Lughnasadh, on August 1, are the quarter marks of the year. Other sabbats are held to mark the summer and winter solstices and the spring and fall equinoxes.

Wiccans meet more frequently than eight times a year, however. Their regularly scheduled meetings—usually held during every full moon—are known as esbats. The esbat ritual typically follows a certain pattern. First, the meeting place is consecrated, usually by drawing an imaginary circle around the participants with an athame (dagger) or wand. Next, the witches invite the gods to attend. Prayers are offered once the Goddess (or God) is informed of the meeting, and then thanks are given. A ritual known as "Cake and Ale" is performed at this time, which is an acknowledgement of the blessings that have been received. If spells or charms are required, they are performed after Cake and Ale. The ceremony ends with a parting of the gods and closing of the circle.

Magick

Witches define magick (spelled with a "k" by witches to differentiate it from the sleight-of-hand performed by stage magicians) as the "art of making changes in reality by acts of Will and Imagination."[14] Witches believe that, with the proper instruction, anyone can perform magick, although its power and effectiveness will depend on the strength of the witch's belief and will. Witches make magick using their psychic abilities, the forces of nature, and certain objects, such as wands, candles, plants and herbs, amulets, and crystals. However, according to witches, the greatest instrument of magick is the power of the mind.

Witches also assert that magick in and of itself is neither good nor bad; it is the witch's intent that determines the outcome of the spell. Just as spells to help someone (known as white magick) are real, so too are spells cast with an evil intent (known as black magick), they claim. Because spells can be affected by one's moods, witches who follow the Wiccan Rede and the Rule of Three are wary of casting spells when they are angry, jealous, or feeling vengeful. However, witches do not cast only beneficial spells. Some witches make black magick because they are not intimidated by the Rule of Three or do not care. As witch Gerina Dunwich writes in her book *Exploring Spellcraft*, "black magick has always been, and most likely will always be, practiced throughout the world." For those who might scoff at the idea of witches and magick, Dunwich adds that black magick is a real force that can harm someone. She warns her readers:

> It is foolish to deny its existence and naïve to believe that any guardian spirit, angel, or god or goddess of your choice will always watch over you and keep you safe from harm. This is akin to believing that a loaded gun cannot possibly harm you because you have convinced yourself that the gun does not exist and therefore has no power over you. You are only fooling yourself.[15]

Nearly every book on witchcraft includes a chapter on spells, but few, if any, include instructions on how to seek revenge or place a curse or hex on an enemy. Most spell books will, however, provide information on how witches can protect themselves if they have been the target of black magick.

Regardless of whether one takes the Rule of Three seriously, it is easy to see why the theory of magick and witchcraft exerts a strong pull on witches and nonwitches alike. As Robert Todd Carroll writes in his *Skeptic's Dictionary*, "The idea of being able to control such things as the weather or one's health by an act of will is very appealing. So is the idea of being able to wreak havoc on one's enemies without having to lift a finger: just think it and thy will will be done."[16]

Despite witches' belief in the power of their spells, science has been unable to prove the existence or efficacy of magick. Witches, for their part, offer several explanations for why a spell may not appear to work. For one thing, it may take time for a spell to take effect. Dunwich mentions that the results of one spell did not appear until a year and a day after the spell was cast. And sometimes spells fail to work. Factors that can affect a spell's success or failure are, according to Dunwich, the witch's willpower, her skill in visualizing the results she wants, and lunar and planetary influences. In addition, she writes that a spell may not work if it is not performed properly, if the witch is feeling ill or does not have the appropriate energy to cast a spell, or if another witch is working against the spell.

In short, there is a ready excuse to explain why a spell did not achieve the desired result. If there are many reasons to explain why a spell did not work, it is also possible to attribute the success of a spell to coincidence. In any case, most consequences of the spells witches cast have readily explainable causes that have nothing to do with magick.

In modern times, the controversy over witchcraft is still due to beliefs about witches' relationship with the devil. Some people, mostly Christian conservatives, still consider witches to be the devil's agents, much as Christians did hundreds of years ago. They believe that witches have signed away their souls in pacts with the devil and that witches are a threat to them and to Christianity. On the other hand, even the Catholic Church itself takes a more moderate position regarding the supposed relationship between witches and the devil. Theologian Herbert Thurston writes that, while the *possibility* of a witch making a pact with the devil cannot be dismissed out of hand, a review of the literature shows that 99 percent of the convictions for witchcraft were based solely on the cruelties of torture and self-delusion.

Witches, of course, deny all charges of devil worship, claiming that their religion is a joyous, peaceful one that centers on the Goddess and nature. The acknowledged tenets of witchcraft do not accept a belief in the devil, so it is unlikely that witches would worship him. However, as is true for almost every belief, there may be a few witches who break away from their religion's stated doctrine and practice black magick with the help of some gods and goddesses that could be classified as "demonic." As has always been the case, the evil done in the name of organized religion is of human, not divine origin.

Notes

1. Quoted in Time-Life Books, *Witches and Witchcraft.* Alexandria, VA: Time-Life Books, 1990, p. 44.
2. Quoted in Carol F. Karlsen, *The Devil in the Shape of a Woman: Witchcraft in Colonial New England.* New York: Norton, 1998, p. 9.
3. Quoted in Time-Life Books, *Witches and Witchcraft*, pp. 44–46.
4. Quoted in Time-Life Books, *Witches and Witchcraft*, p. 72.
5. Quoted in Karlsen, *The Devil in the Shape of a Woman*, p. 137.
6. Quoted in Karlsen, *The Devil in the Shape of a Woman*, p. 138.
7. Quoted in Karlsen, *The Devil in the Shape of a Woman*, p. 141.
8. Silver RavenWolf, *Teen Witch: Wicca for a New Generation.* St. Paul, MN: Llewellyn, 1998, p. 4.
9. Margot Adler, *Drawing Down the Moon: Witches, Druids, Goddess-Worshippers, and Other Pagans in America Today.* Rev. ed. New York: Arkana, 1997, p. 62.
10. Raymond Buckland, *Witchcraft from the Inside: Origins of the Fastest Growing Religious Movement in America,* St. Paul, MN: Llewellyn, 1995, pp. 31–32.
11. RavenWolf, *Teen Witch*, p. 8.
12. Quoted in Lady Sabrina, *Exploring Wicca: The Beliefs, Rites, and Rituals of the Wiccan Religion.* Franklin Lakes, NJ: New Page Books, 2000, pp. 25–26.

13. Quoted in Silver RavenWolf, *To Ride a Silver Broomstick: New Generation Witchcraft*. St. Paul, MN: Llewellyn, 1999, p. 270.

14. Quoted in Lady Sabrina, *Exploring Wicca*, p. 153.

15. Gerina Dunwich, *Exploring Spellcraft: How to Create and Cast Effective Spells*. Franklin Lakes, NJ: New Page Books, 2001, p. 184.

16. Robert Todd Carroll, "Magick," *Skeptic's Dictionary*, last updated October 5, 2001. www.skepdic.com.

Organizations to Contact

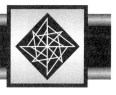

The editors have compiled the following list of organizations concerned with the issues debated in this book. The descriptions are derived from materials provided by the organizations. All have publications or information available for interested readers. The list was compiled on the date of publication of the present volume; the information provided here may change. Be aware that many organizations take several weeks or longer to respond to inquiries, so allow as much time as possible.

American Family Foundation (AFF)
PO Box 413005, Naples, FL 34101-3005
(941) 514-3081 • fax: (941) 514-3451
e-mail: infoserv@affcultinfoserve.com
website: www.csj.org

AFF is a secular research organization that studies psychological manipulation and cults. Its mission is to educate the public and help those who have been adversely affected by participation in a cult. It publishes the research journal *Cultic Studies Journal*, the newsletter *Cult Observer*.

Christian Research Institute (CRI)
PO Box 7000, Rancho Santa Margarita, CA 92688-7000
56051 Airways PO, Calgary, Alberta T2E 85K Canada
(949) 858-6100 • fax: (949) 858-6111
Canada: (800) 665-5851

The CRI seeks to encourage orthodox, biblical Christianity. The CRI disseminates information on cults, the occult, and other religious movements whose teachings and practices are inconsistent with the institute's biblical views. The institute publishes the *Christian Research Journal*, the *Christian Research Newsletter*, and the articles "What About Halloween?" and "The Hard Facts About Satanic Ritual Abuse," among others.

Council of the Magickal Arts (CMA)

PO Box 6756, Abilene, TX 79608-6756
e-mail: cma@magickal-arts.org
website: www.magickal-arts.org

The CMA is an association that promotes spirituality based on pagan beliefs. The council sponsors religious programs and festivals for its members to celebrate pagan holidays. Its quarterly magazine, *Accord*, is devoted to the religion and practice of Wicca and other magical arts.

Covenant of the Goddess (COG)

PO Box 1226, Berkeley, CA 94701
e-mail: info@cog.org • website: www.cog.org

The Covenant of the Goddess is an international organization of Wiccan covens and solitary practicing Wiccans. COG was formed to provide and ensure witches receive the legal protection they are guaranteed under the U.S. Constitution. The organization sponsors an annual summer meeting and festival, encourages networking among its members, issues ministerial credentials to qualified witches, and publishes *Covenant of the Goddess Newsletter*.

Cult Awareness Network (CAN)

1680 N. Vine, Suite 415, Los Angeles, CA 90028
(800) 556-3055 • fax: (323) 468-0562
e-mail: can@cultawarenessnetwork.org
website: www.cultawarenessnetwork.org

CAN's primary goal is to promote religious freedom and the protection of religious and civil rights. CAN gathers information about diverse groups and religions, maintains an extensive reference database, and sponsors conferences open to the public. The network also staffs a national hotline for individuals who are concerned that their friends or relatives may be involved with a questionable religious group. CAN publishes a newsletter periodically as well as a variety of brochures and booklets on religious conversions, belief systems, lifestyles, and related issues.

Ontario Consultants on Religious Tolerance

PO Box 514, Wellesley Island, NY 13640-0514
Box 27026, Frontenac PO, Kingston, Ontario K7M 8W5
Canada
fax: (613) 547-9015
website: www.religioustolerance.org

The Ontario Consultants on Religious Tolerance is composed of a small group of volunteers who provide accurate information about minority religions (including Wicca), religious fraud, hatred, and current religious topics. It hopes its efforts to counter misinformation spread by others will lead to understanding and tolerance and decrease bigotry. The organization presents, compares, and contrasts all sides of each issue in its publications, such as "Teenagers and Wicca" and "Is Wicca a Form of Satanism?"

Spiritual Counterfeits Project (SCP)

PO Box 4308, Berkeley, CA 94704
(510) 540-0300 • (510) 540-1107
e-mail: access@scp-inc.org • website: www.scp-inc.org

SCP is a Christian ministry that monitors spiritual trends, including cults, the occult, Eastern religions, and the New Age movement. The organization maintains an extensive library with files on cults and new religious movements and offers films, tapes, leaflets, outreach services, and counseling to the public. Its publications include the *SCP Newsletter* and the *SCP Journal*, as well as a variety of books and educational materials.

Watchman Fellowship

PO Box 13340, Arlington, TX 76094
(817) 277-0023 • fax: (817) 277-8098
website: www.watchman.org

The Watchman Fellowship specializes in the study of new religious movements, including cults, the occult, and the New Age movement. The organization researches claims of questionable cult practices and provides counseling for former cult members. It offers several articles, videotapes, and books on Satanism, and publishes the *Watchman Expositor* magazine.

Wiccan Church of Canada (WCC)

509 St. Clair Ave. W., PO Box 73599, Toronto, Ontario
M6C 1C0 Canada
(416) 656-6564
e-mail: info@wcc.on.ca • website: www.wcc.on.ca

The Wiccan Church of Canada strives to help practicing Wiccans achieve a spiritual balance with their gods. The church also strives to raise public awareness about the true nature and beliefs of Wicca and paganism, and works to ensure that its members receive the same legal protections and benefits enjoyed by other religions. Its website contains a recommended reading list concerning all aspects of Wicca and paganism.

Witches' League for Public Awareness (WLPA)

PO Box 909, Rehoboth, MA 02769
e-mail: hernesson@aol.com • website: www.celticcrow.com

The league was formed in 1986 to educate the public and provide correct information about witches and witchcraft. The WLPA website contains many links and archived articles and editorials culled from the Internet and other sources about witches, pagans, Wicca, and other subjects of interest to witches.

The Witches' Voice

PO Box 4924, Clearwater, FL 33758-4924
website: www.witchvox.com/wvoxhome.html

The Witches' Voice is an online news and educational network and Internet search engine with over thirty-six hundred Web pages and forty-one thousand links to information on witches, Wicca, and pagans. The website also features monthly essays for teens and adults about witches, Wicca, and related topics.

For Further Research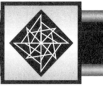

Books

Margot Adler, *Drawing Down the Moon: Witches, Druids, Goddess-Worshippers, and Other Pagans in America Today.* Rev. ed. New York: Arkana, 1997.

Amber K, *Covencraft: Witchcraft for Three or More.* St. Paul, MN: Llewellyn, 1998.

Armed Forces Chaplains Board, *Wiccan Religious Background Paper*, May 1998. www.milpagan.org.

David V. Barrett, *Sects, "Cults," and Alternative Religions: A World Survey and Sourcebook.* London: Blandford, 1998.

J.H. Brennan, *Magick for Beginners: The Power to Change Your World.* St. Paul, MN: Llewellyn, 1999.

Raymond Buckland, *Gypsy Witchcraft and Magic.* St. Paul, MN: Llewellyn, 1998.

———, *Practical Candleburning Rituals.* St. Paul, MN: Llewellyn, 1999.

———, *Witchcraft from the Inside: Origins of the Fastest Growing Religious Movement in America.* Revised 3rd ed. St. Paul, MN: Llewellyn, 1995.

Laurie Cabot with Tom Cowan, *Power of the Witch: The Earth, the Moon, and the Magical Path to Enlightenment.* New York: Delta, 1990.

Wade Davis, *The Serpent and the Rainbow.* New York: Touchstone, 1997.

Gus Di Zerega, *Pagans and Christians: The Personal Spiritual Experience.* St. Paul, MN: Llewellyn, 2001.

Gerina Dunwich, *Exploring Spellcraft: How to Create and Cast Effective Spells*. Franklin Lakes, NJ: New Page Books, 2001.

Bill Ellis, *Raising the Devil: Satanism, New Religions, and the Media*. Lexington: University Press of Kentucky, 2000.

Marc Galanter, *Cults: Faith, Healing, and Coercion*. 2nd ed. New York: Oxford University Press, 1999.

Raven Grimassi, *Encyclopedia of Wicca and Witchcraft*. St. Paul, MN: Llewellyn, 2000.

————, *The Wiccan Mysteries: Ancient Origins and Teachings*. St. Paul, MN: Llewellyn, 1997.

Charles George Hebermann et al., eds., *The Catholic Encyclopedia: An International Work of Reference on the Constitution, Doctrine, Discipline, and History of the Catholic Church*. Vol. 15. New York: Encyclopedia Press, 1913.

Michael Jordan, *Witches: An Encyclopedia of Paganism and Magic*. London: Kayle Cathie, 1998.

Stuart A. Kallen, *Witches*. San Diego: Lucent Books, 2000.

Carol F. Karlsen, *The Devil in the Shape of a Woman: Witchcraft in Colonial New England*. New York: Norton, 1998.

Lady Sabrina, *Exploring Wicca: The Beliefs, Rites, and Rituals of the Wiccan Religion*. Franklin Lakes, NJ: New Page Books, 2000.

Bob Larson, *Larson's Book of Spiritual Warfare*. Nashville: Thomas Nelson, 1999.

Walter Martin, *The Kingdom of the Cults*. Rev. ed. Minneapolis: Bethany House, 1997.

Bill Mers and David Wimbish, *The Dark Side of the Supernatural*. Minneapolis: Bethany House, 1999.

Silver RavenWolf, *Teen Witch: Wicca for a New Generation.* St. Paul, MN: Llewellyn, 1998.

———, *To Ride a Silver Broomstick: New Generation Witchcraft.* St. Paul, MN: Llewellyn, 1999.

Elizabeth Reis, ed., *Spellbound: Women and Witchcraft in America.* Wilmington, DE: Scholarly Resources, 1998.

Peggy Saari, *Witchcraft in America.* Elizabeth M. Shaw, ed. Detroit: UXL, 2001.

Richard Smoley and Jay Kinney, *Hidden Wisdom: A Guide to the Western Inner Traditions.* New York: Penguin, 1999.

Wendy Stein, *Witches: Opposing Viewpoints.* San Diego: Greenhaven Press, 1995.

Montague Summers, *Witchcraft and Black Magic.* Detroit: Omnigraphics, 1990.

Time-Life Books, *Witches and Witchcraft.* Alexandria, VA, 1990.

Periodicals

Charlotte Allen, "The Scholars and the Goddess," *Atlantic Monthly,* January 2001.

Christianity Today, "Why We Like Harry Potter," January 10, 2000.

Current Events, "Banning Harry Potter," October 13, 2000.

Catherine Edwards, "Wicca Casts Spell on Teen-Age Girls," *Insight on the News,* October 25, 1999.

———, "Wicca Infiltrates the Churches," *Insight on the News,* December 6, 1999.

S.C. Gwynne-Killeen, "I Saluted a Witch," *Time,* July 5, 1999.

David Keim, "Parents Push for Wizard-Free Reading," *Christianity Today,* January 10, 2000.

P.G. Maxwell-Stuart, "The Emergence of the Christian Witch," *History Today*, November 2000.

Anna Mulrine, "So You Want to Be a Teenage Witch?" *U.S. News & World Report*, March 1, 1999.

Eric Scheske, "Dark Shadows of Turning," *Touchstone*, March/April 1999.

Roger Scruton, "The Rise of Neo-Paganism," *National Review*, September 27, 1999.

Andrew Stuttaford, "Strange Brew," *National Review*, July 12, 1999.

Tim Unsworth, "Aerial Sports and Harry's Magic Around Every Corner," *National Catholic Reporter*, September 1, 2000.

Lauren F. Winner, "Good News for Witches," *Christianity Today*, October 23, 2000.

Index

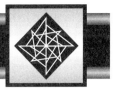